God Didn't Have to Make the Crickets Sing

A Gripping True Story

GAIL CARPENTER

WESTBOW
PRESS
A DIVISION OF THOMAS NELSON
& ZONDERVAN

Copyright © 2014 Gail Carpenter.

All rights reserved. No part of this book may be used or reproduced by any means, graphic, electronic, or mechanical, including photocopying, recording, taping or by any information storage retrieval system without the written permission of the publisher except in the case of brief quotations embodied in critical articles and reviews.

Scripture taken from the Holy Bible, NEW INTERNATIONAL VERSION®. Copyright © 1973, 1978, 1984 by Biblica, Inc. All rights reserved worldwide. Used by permission. NEW INTERNATIONAL VERSION® and NIV® are registered trademarks of Biblica, Inc. Use of either trademark for the offering of goods or services requires the prior written consent of Biblica US, Inc.

WestBow Press books may be ordered through booksellers or by contacting:

WestBow Press
A Division of Thomas Nelson & Zondervan
1663 Liberty Drive
Bloomington, IN 47403
www.westbowpress.com
1 (866) 928-1240

Because of the dynamic nature of the Internet, any web addresses or links contained in this book may have changed since publication and may no longer be valid. The views expressed in this work are solely those of the author and do not necessarily reflect the views of the publisher, and the publisher hereby disclaims any responsibility for them.

The names of many people have been changed to protect their identity and privacy.

Any people depicted in stock imagery provided by Thinkstock are models, and such images are being used for illustrative purposes only. Certain stock imagery © Thinkstock.

ISBN: 978-1-4908-3618-8 (sc)
ISBN: 978-1-4908-3619-5 (hc)
ISBN: 978-1-4908-3617-1 (e)

Library of Congress Control Number: 2014907918

Printed in the United States of America.

WestBow Press rev. date: 07/31/2014

This book is dedicated to my loving husband who so faithfully led, worked and persevered through many trials for the welfare of our family.

Prologue: The Crickets' Song

Last night, while I was relaxing and watching TV, I heard crickets' sounds – or was it one cricket - singing his delightful and confident chirp. The night was a gorgeous, hot and humid August night, and all the windows were open. As I sat and pondered, I kept hearing the distinct, melodic tune.

"That sounds like it's coming from inside the house."

I got up and began my search for the little musician. I followed the song like the Pied Piper to the front door. Carefully, I looked behind the opened door.

There he was – black, shiny and very scared. The music stopped – the wonderful solo that I had enjoyed was silent. He was suddenly hiding in the corner – alone - and, no doubt, worried and insecure about my unexpected presence. It struck me as sad.

He frantically hopped around in the corner trying to escape this hostile ordeal. He was alone and vulnerable, hopelessly trying to make his way out of a dreadful situation. He was a picture of me. I couldn't help but think about all those threatening times that life came crashing down on me, those feelings of panic and despair, of darkness, of feeling alone and confused – hopeless - when I tried to hide in a corner.

This cricket was helpless, at the mercy of my decision to save or kill his life. This precious critter who gave me so much melody stopped singing. He needed some real help. He knew that he could have easily been stomped, squished, destroyed and trashed - flushed down the toilet. And without someone with a caring heart who understood the value of this musician, that fate was the most likely outcome.

I got a broom and gently helped him out the door, back into his freedom, peace, and safety - his natural world - the place where he belonged. His crisis had ended safely just as mine had so many times before, and I felt good about enabling this creature to go back and do what he was supposed to do – sing for me.

After this adventure, I knew it was time for me to share my story of my faithful Father, Rescuer and Savior – the One who saved me from my sins at the cross of Calvary so many years ago and who so lovingly saved me from many threatening trials in my life. The One who helped me deal with all my fears, anxieties and insecurities. I titled my book: *God Didn't Have to Make the Crickets Sing* because it is true. God could have designed each of our nights to be still, dark and quiet.

Now, I love to hear the crickets sing at night. It is such a lovely source of peace and comfort for me to hear their melody trilling through the windows in many amazing crescendos. The songs penetrate the house, the yard, the nighttime as perfect harmony travels for enjoyment, tickling the ears of anyone who will listen. It begins at dusk and carries on regardless of the heat, humidity or the mood I am in – singing to me:

"All is well."
"This is for you."
"I know that you are there, Gail."
"You are not alone."
"Gail, you are precious to Me."
"I understand."
"Gail, I love you."
"I have my crickets singing just for you."

And I am left with a spiritual sense of peace and wonder, a beautiful reassurance of my Heavenly Father's intimate love and giving to all His creation and to me.

What would it be like if the crickets didn't sing at night? Well, I suppose we wouldn't know any differently. You don't know what you don't have, but the richness of this blessing is missed by most and enjoyed by few as God expresses His glory and how far He will go to love us. These wonderful creatures have entertained me for years as I lie in bed at night listening and wondering about the fears and vulnerabilities that have faced my life.

But I didn't always hear them.

As I got a broom and gently helped this cricket back outside to his world of freedom, safety and familiarity, he was going back to his natural home. I was reminded that this is not my true home and sometimes God has to get a broom to gently get me out of a scrape and back onto my path in His loving arms of protection and safety – heading towards my natural home - with Him.

Chapter 1

Surprise!

"Yes, you are pregnant. You're going to have a baby."

Shock and disbelief said, "What! Are you sure? But I'm 41 years old! I can't be pregnant."

So was the beginning of my life. My mother, ready to marry off my 20-year old sister, found out she was with child - with me.

"Well, I'd just get an abortion!" said a well-meaning friend to my mom.

"Oh, I would never do that," retorted my mom, and so I was saved.

Someone get the pacifier!

As my father was passing out cigars and celebrating his virility, my mother was truly having a midlife crisis. It took some time for everyone to get used to my diapers, my bottles, my three months of colic and my commanding presence in the house - what it would mean to start all over again for a mother who was an only child and had previously spaced her two children five years apart. She was almost done raising children and ready for them to leave the nest. Don't get me wrong, my mother was loving and good to me - a great mom - but her shock had to be quite unsettling for a time.

My sister, Ann, was 20 and engaged to be married the year after my birth. Hank, my brother, was 15 and a lanky teenager. My mom had raised her family and then one night –whoops! - an unprotected, unsuspected fling, and God decided I was to be born into the Richardson family.

I was born into an upper middle-class family, a family of stability, love and dedication. My father had recently moved and settled the family to accept a desirable banking position with many opportunities coming his way. My mother's role was supporting my father and maintaining our home, a *Leave it to Beaver* mom for sure. They loved each other and by the time of my birth, they had reached a desirable measure of success and were settling in to enjoy the fruits of that position at the bank and, most likely, looking forward to some freedom.

My mom and dad were a lot of fun:
friendly
teasing
cracking jokes
enjoying good conversation
enjoying life
successful

Now, they were getting adjusted to the idea of caring for me – their new prize. They had lots of social friends – they were social. We enjoyed "the good life."

My dad was like a god to me, powerful, handsome, confident, stable and upbeat. I felt loved and protected by him – safe and sound. I held a healthy respect for him, wouldn't cross him. I knew what switches were. I also knew my dad held his emotions inside. I was a lot like him.

My mother was there for me, caring and nurturing. Unfortunately for her, she had to balance this new maternal calling with her current, appealing station in life of being middle-aged and enjoying the social blessings of my dad's success - the parties, the bridge clubs, the dances at the country club and the hospital twigs.

My grandparents lived far away and seemed especially uncomfortable - a bit scary to me; they were old - old enough to be my great-grandparents - and were not especially affectionate. I just didn't see them that often and, as a result, did not know them very well. They lived in Virginia, and I dreaded going to visit. It was a long, boring drive in the car from Ohio. There was nothing to look forward to. There was no TV and really nothing to do for two to three days while the folks visited. Their house was pleasant and nice but appeared very dark, drab, dated and dull. Coming home after a weekend visit was a breath of fresh air to me after the long drive home from Virginia. I looked forward to going back home during the whole visit.

They seemed very old to me. As I grew up, I saw them age and lose their mental capacities, and I just didn't have any treasured, pleasant memories of visiting them at all:

My memories included:

- visiting my paternal grandmother in her nursing home who did not recognize anyone but my dad
- my grandfather's missing right thumb
- a rather dark home without a TV or something to keep a kid like me entertained
- my maternal grandfather, again with dementia, lying silently - bedridden - in his bedroom

Because of the social obligations of my mom and dad, I spent a fair amount of time with babysitters - some I liked, some I didn't, some stern and some friendly. They were all respectable, older ladies with good references, but, again, these experiences were not always pleasant or comfortable for me – painful. They were not my family, and it left a terrible feeling of abandonment inside me as I watched my mom and dad leave the house smiling together; it felt awful.

My relationship with my brother and sister was always one of age differences, distance and excitement when I looked so forward to seeing them and spending time with them and their families when they came home to visit my folks. My sister married an army guy shortly after I was born, and, soon, she was gone to Austria for three years. I became an aunt at the tender age of three. My brother was still living at home three years after I was born. I remember him coloring with me in coloring books and taking me to get my first pizza during a babysitting escapade at Buckeye Lake. I loved him. He wanted to be with me, at least that's how it made me feel. He left for college at 18, and I was without another sibling at home from then on. When he announced his engagement a few years later, I felt resentment, rejection and pain again.

Empty stanzas for my crickets' song were being formed in my life – in my heart – all those times of feeling fear, insecure, abandoned and the sting of death that I was experiencing as a little girl.

God was preparing a place:
in my heart for Him
where He would fill all my anxieties
that would provide a hope and a presence with me for
    all my days
of peace
to fill my heart with His amazing warmth and love

I can't say that I thought about God much when I was little. But old age and death were very real to me, hard to understand and scary for one so young. I do remember that Esther, our next door neighbor, was taking care of her elderly mother in her home. I had never seen her. One day her mother died, and I recall my mother telling me that "the angels came and took her mother to Heaven." I thought about that as I gazed over at Esther's house wondering how the angels got her mom through the roof!

God Didn't Have to Make the Crickets Sing

My childhood was happy with a few friends and neighborhood kids to play with, understanding and loving parents and a poodle pet named Babs. I was a typical good girl growing up – awkward, with buck teeth – one of only two girls who needed braces in the whole 6th grade! I grew to be 5'9", not real popular and longed for that acceptance and adoration from my peers to satisfy my feelings of abandonment causing my fears and insecurities. I was sure that no one wanted to be with me as much as I wanted to be with them. I usually was the initiator in my friendships. I lived to play with my friends – to have someone want to spend time with me.

I went to church – can't say I got much out of it - didn't like Sunday school, didn't understand about all those Israelites. I liked *The Ten Commandments* movie and had a soft spot in my heart for Jesus. In the movies, He seemed so loving - accepting of everyone - like He might want to spend time with me. He touched my heart.

I didn't know much about crickets as a little girl, but they were there faithfully singing and chirping each summer night.

But inside, I began to:
feel afraid
feel rejected
think I would never get married
feel abandoned
feel left out
have feelings that were painful, oh, so painful

It didn't make sense. I was privileged, loved and protected by my parents and family, but the lies had been embedded in my heart by the enemy that I was missing out and would never find true acceptance and happiness – that it came from the world –not God. I had a big hole in my heart that only God could fill.

God in His wisdom knew just what He was doing in my life. Many spaces were being created for me to cry out to Him.

I didn't realize it at the time, but the emotions of pain and abandonment that were developing in my heart would surface later in my life as I walked my path. God was still there loving me, watching over me and longing to touch my heart with His love.

One day, I would hear the chorus of crickets in my backyard on a summer evening as I lingered on my back porch.

Growing up, I just tried to do well in school, get that boyfriend to love me and please my parents. I knew I had done some wrong things:

stealing

lying

and the typical trouble with mom and dad. I became a normal teenager developing in my own world unaware of God's love and death for me - a God who wanted to reach me and be in a personal relationship with me. I had no clue that my life was soon to change at a simple slumber party.

Chapter 2

The Slumber Party

> In reply Jesus declared, "I tell you the truth, no one can see the kingdom of God unless he is born again." John 3:3

I didn't realize that, very soon, I was going to have an encounter with the living God, the God who loved me. I was 14.

Mom, Dad and I moved to Krebs Addition when I was ten and in the 4th grade. My dad wanted to build his "estate" farther out from the city and our new and modest middle-class home was lovely and nice. Our new house was surrounded by barren fields and a few new houses. The development was still growing, and most of the houses were not constructed yet; I spent my time hanging around some neighborhood kids that I didn't really relate to – some younger, some older, mostly boys – and not too many kids at that. There was no best friend for me down the street.

I went to a new school and made a new friend, a good friend, but she lived far enough away that we didn't get together except occasionally on the weekends. I mainly saw her at school, and we talked on the phone. She also was new to the school and very pretty which attracted much attention from the other kids. She seemed to fit in right away, especially with the boys. I just kind of tagged along, but we did become best friends.

Three years later, I was so excited to hear my mother's words and, hopefully, meet some new, good friends - meet my need for further acceptance.

"Someone told me that there's a new girl moving into the neighborhood. I think there might even be two girls about your age moving up the hill," my mother mentioned in passing one afternoon during summer break.

I was obviously very excited.
Hurray! Ready, set, go –

I was off! In my neediness, I was looking for the song – not hearing it yet. Within the hour, I hopped on my bike and pedaled up the hill hoping to meet my new friends, Karen and Nancy. What luck! I wouldn't be so lonely and bored anymore.

I found the right house only to discover that Karen had not moved in yet. I was directed up the street, three more houses up, to find Nancy. Immediately, I jumped on my bike and rode up to the brick house, knocked on the door and met a life-long friend who was my age. She was friendly, sweet and she liked Barbies! We immediately spent some time together getting to know each other.

"Have you met the other new girl?" I asked with curiosity.

She hadn't. In a few more days, I met Karen riding her bike down by my house at dusk, as I was walking my dog.

"Hi, is your name Karen?" I asked the unfamiliar face pedaling past me.

And from that point on, I bonded with them both and enjoyed two best friends for life. We were inseparable - laughing, playing and riding bikes. I was happy and feeling blessed, but I didn't know the true Source of it - not yet.

As we were goofing around waiting for summer vacation to end, I suggested, "Let's have a slumber party at my house."

It was planned – the food, the fun and the festivities. The festivities were simple - listening to music, playing monopoly, baking cookies and just hanging out, savoring our new-found friendship and talking to the wee hours of the night.

On Friday night, we had the slumber party at my house. By midnight, we were lying on the floor in our sleeping bags talking. Nancy was asleep. I don't even know how the subject came up, but Karen softly said, "Jesus is coming back again - to Israel - and if He is not your Savior, you're not going to be with Him."

"What! He is!"

Shock!! I had *never* heard this before.

It hit me like a:
sledge hammer
brick on my head
shove to the ground
rug being pulled out

This was important, very important! Why was no one paying any attention to God? Why had my parents not told me this? I had gone to church for years and had never heard this before. My heart was deeply convicted and troubled.

"What do I need to do?" I immediately replied.

"You need to tell God that you know you have sinned. You need to believe that Jesus died, was buried and rose again to pay for all *your* sins. You need to ask Him to save you and give Him your life."

I don't remember whether she told me about hell, but I prayed my prayer immediately and felt very strange afterwards – sort of tense - like the blinders had been taken off my eyes, and I was out of this world with the realization of:

my new truth
my new realm
my new life
my personal God

I was born-again spiritually. For me, the mention of Israel pulled a distant God out of the clouds - oblivion - and made Him *very* real to me. He did relate to today and to my everyday life. He was relevant, real, and I knew I needed Him. It was huge for me – unsettling - a new awareness to say the least. I had found Him, and He knew me; I felt connected to Him but not necessarily loved. I had a healthy fear of God.

I sat on the couch the next day staring out the window in my family room wondering if He came today whether I would really go with Him or be left behind. I carried a real sense of dread, wonder and amazement as I contemplated my life and my accountability to God. Jesus did die for me many years ago; I was certainly glad. I knew I was guilty - couldn't get to Heaven on my own. My unworthiness was a stark reality. This was serious, more serious than any other conversation that I had *ever* had with anyone else in the world. I felt that I needed to hold on tight to Him unaware that He had been holding on to me all along. I didn't feel His love, yet, only fear and intimidation.

I had found the Source of the music, but there was so much to learn before I could hear the song.

Chapter 3

The First Notes

Behind the scenes God was working to replace my fear of Him - my legalistic ideas - with a strong faith and to show me His love and grace. Because of my need, I did not feel acceptance from Him. It all seemed very scary at times. Hell was real and eternal life lasted

forever

and ever

and ever

and ever

and ever

and ever

This was very serious to me – an issue to be taken with extreme importance and consideration.

Then I began straining, trying to write my own cricket notes.

I told my parents what had happened to me, but they didn't seem to understand. They thought it was a phase. I still went to church with them with my eyes opened spiritually now. Church became a frustration:

no discussion of sin

no preaching about the blood
no invitation to receive Christ
no evidence people knew a personal Savior
no inner awareness of the Lord
just a religion – a meaningless routine that people performed on Sunday which didn't touch their hearts

"Mom, the preacher talks like everyone is going to Heaven. You have to receive Jesus as your Savior. All of us have sinned against God. We are never going to be good enough on our own."

I wondered, "If God was real and important, why didn't anyone pay attention to Him?" And I wondered why it was so hard for people to believe in a God who made:

their hands
their two sets of teeth
their elbows bend in just the right place to brush their teeth and hold their babies
three sets of tears for their eye
gravity
a perfectly titled Earth
air pockets inside the chicken's egg so the maturing chick will not die
bees who know how to dance to tell other bees the location of flowers
ducks who know how to sit on their eggs until they hatch
butterflies that come from ugly caterpillars
the perfect balance of nature
crickets that sing at night

The list went on forever. I believed that all God had to say to unbelievers when they met Him was, "See that tree out there? Who made it? And did you see the baby I made from a tiny egg?"

He was so real to me – now!

I began praying for my family every day and witnessing when I had the chance. After all, they had not told me the good news of eternal life. I had to find it out at a slumber party. I carried deep concern over these relationships that I loved.

I felt the pressure of trying to please God with my actions and emotions. I tried to balance loving Jesus with adoring the Beatles when I was sixteen.

"I'll always love Jesus more than Paul McCartney," I recited to myself many times. I even prayed for them.

I considered how to weigh dancing, clothes and TV shows with my Christian walk. The only "Christian" people that I knew from school did not believe in:

short hair for girls
shorts and slacks for girls
TV
dances
movies

I worked hard on my own to keep my "fire" and emotions up from one Billy Graham crusade on television to the next and to maintain my emotional faith.

Karen's grandmother was a joyful, knowledgeable Christian who came to visit Karen a few times a year. When her grandmother came to visit, I would dash up to Karen's as fast as I could with many questions, and I was always very excited to receive her answers. I was just so hungry to know more about this God. She gave me a Bible, and I remember how sacred and powerful that book felt to me - a Book written by God, a Book like no other.

The next year, I went to summer church camp with Karen, her brother and her grandmother in the Pennsylvania mountains. I went forward one evening at a small fireside youth meeting to publically declare my faith in Christ. Romans 10: 9-10 was shared with me – "That if you confess with your mouth, 'Jesus is Lord' and believe in your heart that God raised Him from the dead, you will be saved." This was my first precious scripture. Again, the emotions were raw, spooky as if I had entered another domain– not your typical day at church. My heart was pounding, responding deeply to the Lord Jesus Christ; He and His salvation had become the most important part of my life. I was committed even if "no one joined me" and knew "I still would follow."

But God was still writing my song and supplied Karen's dear grandmother to begin teaching me the wonderful and amazing things about God. She gave me little booklets about:

the Rapture
Hell
angels
Heaven
sin
faith
Satan & demons
the Blood

I loved reading them - sometimes in dread, always in wonder - absorbing a whole new spiritual world of which I was now a member.

She taught me about Israel and what that nation means to our world and to Jesus' return.

"Keep your eyes on Israel," she would say.

I have followed that advice all my life as I watch the nightly news.

Karen and I began a little neighborhood Bible study – sort of a mock church service - with a few friends. I became aware of a deep desire to witness about this Jesus and His death, about end times and His return to snatch us out of this world at any moment. After all, no one had told me about being born-again, and I had been just as clueless as they still were. Israel had become a nation around the year of my birth, and I knew prophecy was being fulfilled right before my eyes. I made a vow that I would always share the gospel with any family member or friend that I became close to.

My song was continuing to take form, but no sweet cricket melody for me – not yet.

I was still very much trying to run my life and please God to gain His love and approval on my own.

Chapter 4

College

In his heart a man plans his course, but the Lord determines his steps. Proverbs 16:9

God used my path in college to begin teaching me about faith, grace, love and guidance. He knew of my search - commitment - and took the lead in helping me begin to hear Him.

I was very excited to go to college. I would lie in bed at night and dream, "I can't wait to go to college. I'm hoping to meet that special Christian guy and get married."

This was a matter of supreme importance to me. We would find each other running across campus to embrace. He would meet all my needs, be my Prince Charming, and we would live happily ever after. That's what all the fairy tales said:

Cinderella

Snow White

Sleeping Beauty

He would meet all my needs for acceptance – this guy of mine - and prove that I was worthy of his love.

I was glad high school was over with all the hurts of:

no real boyfriend

no proms
no real dates
no homecomings
no real popularity
being too tall

I was starting over – a clean slate. This would be it. No baggage from the past. I had a plan.

Ready, set, go –
my hair looked great
my clothes were right
pledge the right sorority
meet new people
no more immature boys

I was going to make it and be in bliss in my dream – in my college life:
boys would be interested
I would find my soul mate
I would become a teacher
I looked at the future with excitement and expectation.

Crickets were singing a beautiful tune outside, but I heard only my own melody.

I really had no clue what I was looking for. I thought my melody was in relationships – family, friends and a husband. Maybe it could be in success and jobs or maybe prestige, the list went on and on. But that hole in my heart was created by God – for God. I was made for Him, to love Him and experience His love for me; I just didn't know it yet.

I packed my bags, and off I went in early September. My parents and I arrived at Bowling Green State University around lunchtime. After eating a quick lunch with Mom and Dad, unpacking, meeting my four roommates and any other appropriate people, I kissed my folks and they reluctantly got in the car waving, "Good Bye," unaware of my true feelings of insecurity.

"Don't forget to write."

"Study hard."
"Let us know if you need any money."
"Come home for a visit once in a while."
"We love you."
Ready, set, go –

I was here, and now my dreams were going to come true. I was going to have a man – that family, that good life – all the things that I believed would make me happy. I had bought the lie that life's answers were in relationships, anything other than my precious Creator. This person was going to meet my every need.

The crickets were invisible that first late-summer night at school, but their melody was loud and clear. I was missing it - not hearing it - just as I was still missing intimacy with the true Lover of my soul, the One who wrote the crickets' song, the One who gave His life for me. Eventually, I would be able to hear the crickets sing - my heart wasn't opened yet.

My freshman year was great:
four friendly roommates
good grades
beautiful campus
a dry place on campus for freshmen to dance and meet
    guys every Friday night
my first kiss on the first night
going through rush
becoming the freshman AWS representative for women
    on campus

A sorority was the tool I would use to finally prove to the world that I was popular and meet my sweetheart – a handsome, tall hunk to sweep me off my feet and make me feel wanted and wonderful. I went through rush and got invited back to all the houses! Wow! See, I knew it. I *was* worthy of acceptance after all.

But only three houses invited me to join their sorority at the final parties, not any of the ones I wanted. I was crushed, dismayed and wounded.

"Why didn't they want me?"
"They told me they liked me."
"This is like high school."
"How could I get my man without the help of a good sorority?"

But as I kept writing my own song, I decided to go through rush again my sophomore year. My dream was still there, and I would be accepted - I just knew it. I was determined to make it happen.

College life was mixed. My freshman year was a lot of fun - not the studying part – but the dancing and meeting guy's part, each day looking, expecting, to meet my special boyfriend. But things did not go so well my sophomore year. I couldn't find a Christian group with interesting people, and I *was* looking. The social life involved going uptown and drinking - I wasn't interested in that. I did meet some interested guys, but not for me – too short. The campus was small, and it seemed like everyone went home on the weekends. I just had to find a way to meet my Knight in Shining Armor that I had read about in those childhood stories of mine.

I did pledge one of the sororities, not any of the ones I really wanted, and I never felt satisfied that I was in the right house. I still longed to be a member of the others – the popular ones. I felt the same old feelings of:

rejection
loneliness
hurt
concern
abandonment
unworthiness
isolation

The dream was not working out – beginning to fade - at least at *that* college. College began my path of awareness that the world was not going to give me the song I longed for – my healing, my acceptance, but God would as He guided and taught me along the way. I was unhappy and frustrated – very needy, but only God knew of my deep despair.

He was still preparing my song - creating a melody from Him in my heart.

Unaware to me, God began to show me His path. One of my sorority sisters asked if I would write a letter to a male friend of hers who was in the navy. I mailed a letter, and we began corresponding for a few months. He seemed likable, tall and interesting with a sense of humor. As I got to know him, I felt a connection with him through his letters. He was facing life - courageously - during the Vietnam War. I admired that. Maybe he was the one. As we kept writing, we made arrangements to meet at The Ohio State University one weekend in Columbus. I made arrangements to stay with an old acquaintance from high school.

In my desperation – maybe he's the one - I traveled to Columbus to meet Bob. But he was a "no show," and I never did hear from him again. That night, I stayed in the dorm room of the girl who had gone home for the weekend – alone. I sat there and wondered about my neediness and social unworthiness.

What did life hold for me?
Would I ever be loved by a guy?
I feel so alone and rejected?
God, where are you?
Why don't people want to be with me?
Was I too tall?

When I got back to Bowling Green, I called the girl to thank her, and she told me a little bit about the life and campus at Ohio State. I had a lot of questions. It sounded strangely appealing – a better place for me than where I was. She was looking for another roommate for the next year in a lovely rooming house - with a pool! It was within easy walking distance, four blocks from the campus. She had already arranged for everything; I just had to sign up and move in that September - a smooth, beautiful plan.

No doubt, God moved my heart, and I decided to transfer to Ohio State my junior year and live with two girls from high school.

I really did not see or understand God and His ways at that time. I just knew that this seemed like the way to go. The campus was:

big with more possibilities
busy with more activity
near Campus Crusade for Christ
closer to home
a more diverse community

In the quest for my dream, I wanted to meet a strong Christian man to become my husband. That search seemed limited to me in my present circumstances at my present college, so it was time for a change. I was still determined to make my dream come true and have that happily-ever-after life. I was still writing my own song and seeking to make it happen. It had seemed so socially painful growing up, and – surely - someone at this huge college was going to change that for me, find me, want me, love me.

Everything for my transfer was in place.

That summer, I was living at home with my parents and working at my dad's bank in the accounting department.

My mom usually watched a local talk show on TV around noon. One day I happened to be in the room while the show was on. It caught my attention because two Campus Crusaders from The Ohio State University were being interviewed by the hostess. The girl was an Ohio State cheerleader and she seemed so:

normal
active
cute

The guy was appealing as well. They just seemed like average college kids that I could relate to, and they spoke about their faith in Jesus Christ and their love and service for Him. I was hooked – bad. This is what I had been looking for!

God Didn't Have to Make the Crickets Sing

September came. I packed up again and moved into my off-campus rooming house at Ohio State. After I was settled in, I immediately called Karen's grandmother to help me find out what "club" these students were in and where they were located. They were Campus Crusaders, and the Crusade House was only four blocks away from my rooming house! What luck – or was it a plan? I went to their meetings two nights a week and another Bible study on Mondays in the Union at the end of my street. I was still so hungry to learn more about God and all the marvelous things that were hidden in His word for me:

Things about:
His love story of salvation
spiritual life
righteousness
wholeness
agape love
grace
people of faith
prophecy
sanctification

As I continued in this fellowship for my remaining two years at Ohio State, I discovered so many wonderful principles that God was teaching me through His word. I learned about agape love – not a feeling – but a selfless action of giving to others. I learned how God's agape love accepted me - unconditionally. There it was, my final acceptance from God, and my heart was satisfied. I didn't have to try to please Him anymore for me to be accepted. I didn't have to muster up emotional strength in order to hang on to God and feel close to Him. I just rested in His acceptance and love for me. I was loved through His Son. I never longed for His acceptance again but rested in His grace.

A note was added to my song.

I discovered faith and learned about walking in the Spirit. I had been filled with His Spirit at my spiritual birth when I was

14 and now trusted Him to make my path straight. I was learning how to trust Him to guide my life; my spiritual eyes were really being opened.

Prophecy was a huge topic of interest in the early 70's as prophetic books were being written and gaining attention. I had been born in 1949, the time Israel became a nation again. That was exciting to me, and I was full of great anticipation about Jesus' return. It had been a real part of my salvation experience. Jesus was coming back to Jerusalem and for us - any day. I remained concerned for my family – praying fervently.

In the early 70's, college days for me were:
rioting students
National Guard killing Kent State kids
students throwing bricks at police
being teargased on my street
enjoying Ohio State shutting down for two weeks
studying to become a teacher
learning more of God's word
falling more in love with my Heavenly Father
trusting Him more and more each day with my life
being watched over and protected by my God
finding a deeper relationship with God

But I was still looking for my Knight in Shining armor to meet my deepest emotional needs.

Chapter 5

My Knight in Shining Armor

All-in-all, life was pretty good for me. I loved my major, elementary education. I enjoyed wonderful Bible teaching and had a few friends. But still, no man to love me. I still believed the lie from all those silly love songs that true love and happiness was only in a man:

She loves you
Cherish
We've Only Just Begun
Michelle
If
Can You Feel the Love Tonight?

I was madly searching around each corner. It was important to me – very important. I needed affirmation, didn't want to be alone. I wanted to get married someday, get married to a great guy, a follower of Jesus Christ and someone who would love me and want to be with me – quite a perfect packaged deal.

My mission on the weekends was to go out and meet guys.

"What are you doing this weekend?" I was always asking around.

There were sure lots of opportunities to meet guys at Ohio State, and I planned on taking advantage of each and every one. There was one slight problem - I wanted to find a Christian, a nondrinker, nonsmoker, honorable man. That was going to be tricky at a large state university in the early 70's, not always the most moral place to find my true love.

But God was watching out for me.

One special night, He moved in my life. It was a weekend during the summer after my freshman year. I went to a local club with a friend – looking, looking for my special someone. It was a popular club for the locals to hang out and meet people during the summer. I had fun there and danced plenty. As I sat there watching the beginning of the next dance, I was tapped on the shoulder,

"Do you want to dance?"

I quickly sized him up:

Was he cute?

Was he tall enough?

Was he sober?

Was he a possibility?

"Sure" and my life was changed that night when I met Jeff - my husband. We danced and danced. He was very likeable, funny and cute - in a sort of innocent way - not your typical macho type. I liked him.

He took me home, and we began dating - real ask-me-out kind of dates to:

movies

dances

amusement parks

fairs

just hanging out

God Didn't Have to Make the Crickets Sing

He was very nice, but our backgrounds were very different, and I just wasn't sure. He had a lot of rough edges – sort of trying to find himself. Was he even a Christian? We dated that summer, and I made no commitments.

That winter, Jeff got drafted in the army infantry during the Vietnam War and was very worried about being deployed. I began praying hard about this relationship. I figured I would just know, but I needed to still be open to God. By this point, I knew about trusting God and resting in Him because He had promised to keep me for Himself and work in my life.

We began writing letters. I kept looking to God - wasn't sure. Jeff seemed more vulnerable than what I was comfortable with. My parents became concerned because it seemed like this guy had a ways to go before he was established and could provide a good, stable life for me – not the idea of perfection they were looking for. They began pressuring me. It all became very upsetting and confusing, and I shed many tears of concern trying to find God's plan.

My parents loved me and had a certain type of husband in mind, one with a college degree and similar background to mine. I, also, had these qualities in mind. Jeff was just beginning his path and struggling to obtain the same successes that were dear to me. But it would require a certain degree of faith and commitment to get where he wanted to be. That scared me and threatened my insecurity. But his warm personality, committed love for me and personal goals were starting to grab my heart. I saw the vision with him. We could make a go of it - together:

- tackle the world
- do it right
- get his degree
- get his job
- be in love
- spend time together
- have a family

But I was also concerned about his relationship to God. After all, he would be the father of my children. He would be their spiritual leader. I knew that a person had to have a personal relationship with Jesus Christ. I understood that my religious background in the Methodist Church did not save me – religions don't - and that I had found Jesus Christ at my slumber party. I was not sure he had that relationship, and I kept praying and praying - desperately praying.

Was he the one? I was not very good about making huge life decisions - needed a neon sign in the sky from God. I needed God in a *major* way to show me whether this was right or not. I knew that I was looking for a different life than my parents. I didn't care so much about:

country clubs
status
materialism
social clubs
pride of life
what the world says is important

The lie said, "These were all the answers to life."

I was all about sharing Jesus with people, teaching some 5th graders, getting married and having my little family that I had so longed for. And I was falling deeply in love with this guy.

That next year, I began writing about my relationship with the Lord Jesus Christ and sharing my faith in my letters to Jeff while he was in the army. I told him that he needed to be born-again and give his heart to Jesus. Not a lot of understanding came back, and I was still frantically praying.

Then one day, I began to see God's hand in this relationship. I received a call from Jeff.

"I am not going to Vietnam!! They changed my MOS. A Sergeant saw my insignia on my collar."

The Sergeant asked, "Are you a clerk typist?"

"No, I'm a sports activity specialist."

"Can you type?"

"Yes, I've had two years in high school."

"We're going to send you down to the Pentagon because they need a clerk typist." He explained, "They need a typist at the Pentagon dispensary."

"I am going to Washington D.C. and work in the Pentagon for the rest of my service! I'm not going infantry! I have thanked God and prayed to accept Jesus as my Savior."

FANTASTIC!

UNBELIEVABLE!

PRAYER ANSWER!

HUGE RELIEF!

Thank you, God – another note added to my song.

This blessing enabled Jeff to come home and see me at college. He bought a Ford Falcon and drove home twice a month. He also took some college classes in Washington at a community college to begin his accounting career. He was gaining business experience by working at the Pentagon. God certainly seemed to be leading us together as I was urgently clinging to Him for His plan. I still just didn't know. This was such a big decision for the rest of my life.

But my parents were still pretty disturbed. They were still afraid I was making a mistake. They did not share the faith and values that I depended on.

By the second year, my life became pretty miserable between Jeff and my parents. I was in a lot of pain and confusion about where this was going and what my true feelings were for Jeff. We just didn't get to spend much down-time together, and we were always juggling my feelings about my parents and his feelings of getting serious. I had no intentions of getting married anytime soon because I wanted my degree; my folks were not really listening to me! They were just in fear.

One day at the end of my junior year - out of the blue - Jeff phoned, "Why don't you come out to Washington this next summer and work? My mom has a friend whose daughter works out here. You can stay with her for the summer and find a job."

I thought, "Oh, right! My parents are really going to go along with that."

I began praying - hard. It did seem like a good idea, and then I would know, a chance to be together and to see how I really felt. I was 21 and knew this time together needed to happen for me, for us.

In my seeking, I prayed, "Ok, Father. I'm going to ask my parents and the first words out of their mouth I am going to take as your answer." Maybe not so spiritual, but it was all I had.

When I got the courage, I asked my mom shaking in my shoes, "Jeff wants me to go to Washington and work over the summer. He has a friend that I can live with."

"Oh, sure, go, just take off!" was her sarcastic answer.

I was so torn between both Jeff and my parents that I made a secret appointment with my pastor.

"You are of age and need to find out God's leading," he counseled.

When Mom and Dad found out about my visit, they also made an appointment and talked to Reverend Fisher. After their meeting, they came to me, sat me down and said, "We have been wrong. We won't stand in your way." That brought me more freedom to hear from God.

It was set. But I would need to find a job in Washington. Ready, set, go –

This time with:

more faith

more brokenness

more uncertainty

more expectancy from God

This was a big deal - a very big deal - and a big adventure. I was definitely looking to God about this whole relationship and what He would show me. I didn't have all the answers any more.

I only knew what was developing in my heart; I truly wanted to find God's choice for me, and I was falling in love with Jeff.

That summer between my junior and senior year, I was off to Washington D.C. I had worked in my father's bank in the accounting department for the past two summers, but I was looking for anything. I gave God one week to find a job for me, otherwise I would not believe He was guiding me in this and would return home.

I was full of anticipation when I got to Washington being very comfortable around Jeff, feeling protected by him and feeling lots of his love and his leadership. Jeff met me at the airport and drove us around the city. Then I met the girl and her roommate and got settled in their apartment.

Before I knew it, Monday morning came, and I was taking the bus downtown every morning for a week. I loved the feeling, the excitement, the independence, the adventure and the culture - the city itself:

beautiful
busy
bustling
beckoning
bursting with activity
historical

As I walked down a few streets and began my job search, I heard employers say:

"No, we don't need anyone."

"No, we just hired someone yesterday."

"No, not today."

I found a dress shop that might need someone week nights and weekends, but that defeated the whole purpose of the summer - spending quality time together with Jeff - and this was all about having a chance to be together.

"Hey, Jeff, I don't know if this is going to work out," I worried as the week went on. It didn't look too hopeful. I needed to have a job to pay rent and to help with college living expenses.

Friday morning came and NO JOB! Guess it wasn't to be.

My feelings were numb and discouraging. I gave them to God. I still just didn't know His plan in this.

As I walked along the beautiful streets of downtown Washington D.C. near the White House after lunch, I really didn't know where else to go. I had given up. We had been dating for two years, and I felt that we really did need this time to be together to see how we got along. This long distance relationship was strained, at best, especially when we were dealing with the Vietnam War, upset parents and establishing careers.

It was around 1:00 Friday afternoon. I needed to cash a check to have some money for a plane ticket to fly back home. I found a bank and went up to the teller.

"Can I cash my check?"

"Sorry, this is an out-of-state check. You will have to have it approved by that officer sitting over there."

I looked around over my shoulder. There was a nice-looking, middle-aged gentleman sitting behind his desk in the corner of the bank. He reminded me a bit of my dad. I walked over.

"Excuse me. I am from Ohio, and I would like to cash my check. Can you do this for me?"

He pleasantly complied.

Then my words just came out.

"I am looking for a summer job, and I have experience in banking. Do you have anything?"

"As a matter-of-fact, we just had a girl quit in the accounting department. When could you start?" was his unbelievable reply.

BINGO!

WONDERFUL!

AMAZING!

A MIRACLE!

The last minute and God was in this. I was hired in the accounting department for the rest of the summer. I would work 9:00 to 4:30 five days a week with the weekends off – just what I had been hoping for. It was incredible to me and very, very exciting – a true affirmation of God. My heart was warmed with goose bumps from the top of my head to my tippy-toes with God's love – of this intimate connection to my Creator – stupendous and beyond amazing.

God added more notes as the crickets' chorus was taking form.

Jeff picked me up at 4:00 trying to hold onto hope.

"I didn't find anything," I teased.

Then I shouted, "Yes! Our God is with us in this! I got a job!!" It was quite impressive to both of us - our second blessing to draw us together.

We had a great summer:
visiting monuments
picnicking in the parks
visiting my sister in Hampton, Virginia
playing cards
hanging out
traveling to battle fields
touring Washington D.C.
spending time together

Jeff continued to take college classes two nights a week. We went to church most Sundays. This was important to me - so important. He had to be saved, a believer. God commanded it.

I never did hear any crickets singing in downtown Washington DC that summer. I heard the song about Jeff.

At last, I had found my guy, but I was still writing my own song.

We dated five years in all. He got out of the service. We were married, and he finished his degree at Ohio University while I taught my 5th grade classes.

Now, I had found that love - my knight – the one who had swept me off my feet. I had found the key to all:

my troubles
my happiness
my emotional needs
my acceptance
my loneliness

But it wasn't long before my handsome knight would fall off his horse, and I wouldn't be able to get him back on it again.

Unwittingly, I would someday hear another note of the tune in my broken, needy life.

Chapter 6

Happily Ever After

... My soul glorifies the Lord. Luke 1:46

It is amazing how deceived we can be about the true meaning of life and its promises. We are surrounded by God's creation, the glory and beauty of it all, but we just don't get it – at least, I didn't get it.

Invisible crickets were faithfully playing their choruses of God's love every steamy summer night, and I failed to notice the melody. It was just sounds, noise - part of the evening.

But God sends His love every day of our lives - anyway. We are just so spiritually dead towards Him that we don't realize it until He allows us to face a hurt or a disappointment that comes in life – face the lies that promise us fulfillment and then let us down. Then His song can begin breaking through if we seek our Creator. He uses hurts to prepare our hearts to receive His truth and love. Oh, I believed and had a personal relationship with Jesus, but my deepest awareness and needs were still unmet because I was looking in all the wrong places.

After the wedding, we went to Niagara Falls on our honeymoon and had a wonderful time of love and bonding. We got back and set up a home, a cute apartment, with all the warmth of our love. And then one day right after we got back from our honeymoon, I was told, "I'm going to a ball game tonight. The summer season has started, and we have two practices a week and a game on Saturdays."

"What! And leave me here alone? What about the things we can do together on the weekend? That is a lot of time just for you. What about me? I thought I was the love of your life! Don't you want to be with me? I don't want to sit here alone or watch all those ball games!"

I wasn't prepared for this division. Here it was again – the same experience as before:

rejection

abandonment

loneliness

feeling unloved

Again, I was being left out and watching someone go off and have fun - away from me. This was hard for me to understand and very hurtful. In fact, it was shocking to me. This was not the way we had built this relationship. I didn't know he loved sports. This was not how it was suppose to be. What about all those times we enjoyed together? Weren't they enough? I thought he loved me. I thought we were married and in love as a couple.

Clearly, our expectations were different after our big day had ended and, I am sorry to say, there were many arguments and tears about this issue. We had our share of fiery fights over ball games and practices. Looking back, I don't really blame my husband for this – maybe there was selfishness on his part, maybe I was being selfish too, but I only know that this hurt and hurt a lot. I didn't grow up with brothers and sisters who were close to my age, so I didn't really understand family dynamics. I never had to share my toys with anyone. I got to keep my room just the way I wanted it, and no one messed up my Barbie dolls when I was done playing with them. It was really all about me, but I didn't feel like I was expecting anything wrong at the time. It only seemed emotionally right that two people in love would want to spend any extra time together enjoying each other's company. That's what we did in Washington.

And it felt so:
right
wonderful
fulfilling

Our communication was not the best, very emotional and over-charged with poor listening. We were both young, immature kids starting out trying to get our needs met in ways other than God – deep needs that had built up for both of us over the years. Both of us had experienced rejection in some way, and we could not put our defenses down. It was like my husband had become a stranger and not my best friend in this area, not sharing all his life with me. I'm sure Jeff felt the same way.

Maybe I was too needy – self-focused, but I didn't see it because I had bought the lie in the fairy tales - hook, line and sinker. It made sense to me that when you love someone, you would want to spend time with them and they with you - true love. That was what I had learned. I longed for this relationship to be special. But fantasy can be distorted and deceptive because we have this sin nature:

selfish
self-focused
self-serving
hurtful
prideful

I was as guilty as the rest. I wanted to spend time with someone on my terms. I wasn't too good on the agape, selfless-giving part where I would give to others when I really didn't want to meet their needs at all - only mine. I needed to learn how to do that, and God was beginning to teach me how to love others when they were unlovely and how to love myself when I was unlovely. It really was not all about me, and God was the best example:

"But God demonstrates His own love for us in this: while we were still sinners, Christ died for us." Romans 5:8

He came for me.
He rescued me.
He loved me unconditionally.
He was there for me.
He wanted to spend time with me.
He saved me.
He could change me.
He could give me joy and peace.

Whatever the source of the problem, this area of our marriage caused me a lot of sorrow, bitterness and misunderstanding. We struggled with it for eight long years. It involved both softball and basketball. We did work out a compromise of one game and one practice a week, a treaty that held with a fragile line, but my continued resentment and hurt in this relationship grew deeper and deeper. I just could not get this part of my life right. I didn't know what was wrong.

Jeff and I did love each other very much and did enjoy many good times. But something was missing for me, something that made me still feel separated, alone, unloved and unaccepted. What was it? Was there another Knight?

Chapter 7

Family

Children can be fascinated by crickets - shiny, little black bugs that rub their wings together to make sounds. Children may be too busy to hear the music, but they can marvel at the strange creatures of God's design.

We were married, and our life had begun.

I was teaching 5th grade. I loved my job, and I was good at it. It fit me like a glove because my students seemed to love me, wanted to be with me, wanted me as their teacher, and we just enjoyed our classroom. I had a creative outlet and made my lessons fun and interesting - engaging my kids. My principal said, "You are a natural teacher." I think it was so easy for me because I enjoyed the companionship of my students. This position met a deep need for me of acceptance and love. I spent six engaging years teaching in a county elementary school with staff and three wonderful principals. I enjoyed the job immensely.

Jeff was busy finishing up college on the GI bill in accounting and dreaming all the dreams that go along with that path.

Having children - a family - was high on my list. I was determined to have what I felt I lacked as I grew up. I thought

family was the huge, missing piece of my puzzle of being loved and needed in my life. Idealistically, I had watched other families:
- have fun playing
- be together
- have acceptance
- enjoy companionship
- not be alone with no siblings to create happiness

I didn't feel especially fond of little babies - didn't always have love or patience for those little babysitting, messy babies that I often watched as a teenager. Still, I felt the desire to establish my own family with Jeff. I looked forward to it - family - maybe that was the answer to my deepest needs. Then I would have people want to spend time with me. It would be enough to make me happy.
Ready, set, go -

After five years of marriage, we began trying to have a child in early summer. I entered this part of my life with wonder and a certain sense of trepidation since it was an unknown. Did I even know how to be a mom? Again, I was asked to go into a new adventure with:
- uncertainty
- change
- risk
- hope
- faith

This girl was certainly not the confident girl who went off to college writing my own crickets' song.

I knew I didn't have control over this birth and motherhood thing. Would everything be OK? I felt vulnerable to this unknown experience - childbirth. It was another journey of faith teaching me to trust God. It was very scary to me – the whole birth and all. Some of the stories I had heard, and the attitudes about it were less than calming. Frankly, they were upsetting to me. After all, I had never even gotten my ears pierced because I couldn't imagine how painful that must be, putting a needle through my ears – ouch! But I knew I wanted a family which meant children with childbirth. This was different – a whole new adventure – with no definite answers:

Who would I have?
How much would it hurt?
How would a baby get out of me?
Would the baby be healthy?
Would the baby love me?
Would the baby cry all the time?
Would I enjoy this new role in my life?

I was trying to trust my Heavenly Father to get me through, but not hearing the music each day. For me, the music was now in my children - but the crickets kept right on singing outside my house.

I didn't realize that God had planned my journey by planting deep seeds of faith, trust and risk that would grow for the rest of my life, a pattern of God's faithfulness that I would need to experience, so that I would have the inner strength to face some pretty dark tomorrows. This was a God who had:

promised to be with me
promised He would never leave me
promised to love me
promised to strengthen me
promised to meet all my emotional needs
promised to provide my security
dazzled me
warmed my heart
whispered, "Trust me"

Jeff and I went through Lamaze, and we were totally prepared for childbirth. I knew how to breathe and knew what to expect. Jeff was a great coach. God graciously granted our decision to have a child. A beautiful baby girl was born at 7lbs. 4oz. My insecure feelings about this whole mother-thing just vanished immediately when I saw her and heard her cry. She was so vulnerable, just like I had felt, and I loved her. I was her mom, and I was glad. I wanted this baby and would be there for her. She was a miracle of God, and her cry was very spiritual to me – a new life. She was so:

precious
cute
innocent
vulnerable
sweet

The list could go on and on.

She was a miracle - a typical everyday miracle – a creation of God that most people just miss and take for granted, the wonder of birth. Some people will say:

"I won't believe in God unless I see a miracle or hear Him speak." He *is* speaking loud and clear in birth – this child of mine that came from a tiny egg cell to become a person perfectly formed with fingers, toes, eyelashes, eyelids and nerves that move muscles.

But it is so common - ordinary, everyday - and we miss it, just like the crickets' melodies because we don't see through spiritual eyes; we just don't listen with spiritual ears.

We are spiritually blind. We are spiritually deaf. We take God and His richest blessings for granted as we sail through life unaware of the total dependence we have on Him for all our needs:

food
water
air
the sun shining in the sky
birth
grace
love
ability to work

jobs

Somehow this new role also fit like a glove. She needed me, and I was very fulfilled. I was amazed at how quickly I fit into my new-found position of motherhood with all my heart and soul.

This must be it, what I've been looking for. It feels so wonderful, just like the first feelings I had for Jeff. *Now*, I had found the song. It was in the family I had always longed for:

the fun
the play
the nurturing
the bonding
the care that my children needed

I was there for them, delighting in them - my greatest joy – creating our home.

My other two children were born soon after that, and I felt the same way about their births. I adored them and the time I spent with them. Jeff was a great dad, and our family all seemed so happy and right. I loved watching them grow and learn.

We enjoyed just a great family life of:
riding bikes
playing whiffle ball
bedtime stories, prayers and hugs
taking vacations to the beach
campouts in sleeping bags in the living room on Saturday
    nights
birthday parties
playing games
having friends over
doing school
going to church
laughing
singing
being together

It was wonderful, this life with my kids. I lost myself in trying to be a great mom, and I *was* a great mom just like my mom had been for me. But I had defined it differently. I would be there developing the relationships, and it was right and wonderful almost every minute. These young years were some of the happiest of my life. We were just a very happy bunch clumping around together.

But as the years progressed, my old feelings of abandonment and rejection began to surface as I watched my children grow up and away - not need me as much. They wanted to be with their friends, they had interests outside of my home. I knew this was natural and normal. I knew this was needed, and I expected these changes for my own children as well. But I wasn't prepared for how soon and fast their adulthood seemed to come. I wanted them to be successful and happy in life; I wanted them to know their God and benefit from this personal faith that I was learning about. That relationship for them was very important to me. But it was still very painful when they chose another person to spend time with other than me.

Yet, I had been the same way when I was a teenager. My mom and dad had given me lots of freedom when I grew up. I enjoyed:
lots of slumber parties
meeting the Beatles at 16
getting Paul McCartney's autograph
riding bikes to Frisch's with my friends
going to the movies
going to a few parties
talking for hours and hours on the phone

It's what teenagers do. They weren't doing anything wrong. I know my parents had to feel the same abandonment themselves as they watched their self-absorbed teenager begin to leave their nest. I am sure they felt the same pain in these changes. After all, I had been a second family to them in their later years – keeping

them young. Now, I thought about my mom's possible pain at times. Sometimes she commented about me:
- being in such a hurry to go see my friends
- talking on the phone for hours
- missing dinner

I knew this pattern well from my past. But why did I feel all this pain now? It was just natural. I didn't understand my reactions or pain at that time until God gave me some insight later. But I knew that something really hurt deep inside me as I:
- watched them grow up
- was not able to protect them anymore
- was not the first person chosen to share personal thoughts and feelings

That big hole was getting larger in my heart.

I didn't care anything about crickets and their songs at that point as I struggled with myself and the pain of giving away the most precious people who I passionately loved with a bond that we shared – a heartfelt bond that was my life for years and now was losing to the world.

College for my kids came, and I kissed everyone "Good-bye" excited that they had all made it, and we could pay for it! It was almost a relief, and I was OK with it.

But when they were married, it became quite different – that was the ultimate abandonment of me to someone else; I felt the exact same and total rejection of me in the loss of these dear relationships with my children because it really seemed to be all about everyone else and their joy while I felt terribly left out. My heart was bleeding all over the floor.

When I grew up, my married sister and my brother moved far away, basically, to never see them again other than once a year for a brief visit. When people in my family got married, to me it was:

Good-bye.

We're leaving.

You're done.
We don't care about you anymore.
We don't need you anymore.
See ya 'round.

I felt no real emotional connection to them after that. It was all about their families. I didn't want that distance with my own children. This was going to be painful - very painful. I didn't know if I could do it, and I struggled. I prayed – hard.
Ready . . . set . . . go - at a snail's pace.

I didn't even know if I could go and buy a wedding dress - forget about making it through the first wedding. The dress seemed like a shroud and the ceremony like death. In all my overreaction and feelings of abandonment, I did a terrible job marrying off my first daughter - prayed like crazy that I could just get through the ceremony without breaking down. I did make it through with lots of smiles on my face. Did other moms feel like this? My precious relationship with my girl was ending – over! It would *never* be the same.

Pain, pain and more pain - why so much pain when this was supposed to be a happy time – a celebration?

I was so out-of-control, over-reacting and not trusting God for my children. Watching others involved with my daughters' lives was excruciatingly painful for me. I felt left out – totally rejected. They were *my* daughters! It felt like the times when my brother and his family came for a visit, and I had to send my little dog, Babs, to the babysitters - left out. How would I be part of their lives now?

My friend said, "They have husbands now." That was even *more* painful. It felt like death to me – like my daughters had just died. I didn't want to take away from their relationships with their spouses; I just didn't know how this was ever going to work – how I would fit in as an outsider looking in with my heart breaking. I would return from visits at their homes in tears, not understanding so much of what was going on inside of me. Why was I in so much pain? Where was all this pain coming from? I just didn't understand. I needed some real answers - badly.

The crickets were all dead - no song in my heart - but God was still at work faithfully forming my sweet tune.

It wasn't long before I felt God leading me to ask forgiveness from both of my daughters and their husbands. I knew that I was wrong. I still couldn't figure these feelings out. I had grown up in a loving family, with a loving husband and children. God would soon reveal my secrets and help me overcome them.

Chapter 8

Journeys Begin

You have made known to me the path of life.
Psalm 16:11

So far, life was pretty good for the Carpenters. We were beginning to live the American dream. I was a stay-at-home mom teaching a day and a half at an elementary school around the corner. Keri was staying with a former babysitter of mine, an older lady, in my own home on Mondays and Tuesday mornings. Jeff was doing well in his first accounting job, doing the whole corporate grind with all the big dreams ahead of us. Mom and Dad lived around the corner, and we were all enjoying Keri. I loved our little Cape Cod home and had a blast fixing it up:

wallpapering
painting walls
stenciling
sewing curtains
remodeling the kitchen
gardening

Everything *Better Homes and Gardens* recommended for the perfect, warm and cozy home, I did. I was really into it. This had to be the life that I was looking for – being together as a family with our child. I was so fulfilled, so blessed. I felt warm and fuzzy almost every day.

We were in a great Bible study, going to church on Sundays, living a wonderful life. Many expectations were ahead for Jeff and his career; we would have the American dream:

good, stable job
Leave it to Beaver mom
friends
family
finances
promotions
dreams
retirement

This part felt really good. I thought that we really had it made. We had done it right and now would enjoy the fruit of all our labor. I had convinced myself that our station in life was, perhaps, what I had been searching for all along. Except for a skirmish here and there, life was fantastic. I loved God, was fascinated studying about Him in a good Bible study, but my faith and relationship with God had not really been tested. I was still pretty independent. He was still distant - a belief, a concept - only to learn about and wonder about. But our trials of the past seemed like a foggy memory to get us to this point where things were always going to be just fine. That was soon to change, and I was not prepared at all.

Jeff and I had both grown up with stable fathers who had good, steady jobs. My father had changed jobs a few times, but by the time I came along, he was established - big time - at the bank. Jeff's dad had worked for a coal company for many years as well. Obviously, we expected to work 30 years for a company and retire with that gold watch and pension. Nobody told us about affirmative action and down- sizing in the late 70's and early 80's. What was that anyway?

Jeff expected a promotion from his company in about five years to the main headquarters in Wisconsin, but it came sooner than that. After two years, he was promoted because the opportunity came early, and his boss knew he was ready. This news was very exciting for us – had to be horrendous for my aging folks who lived around the corner. I was oblivious to their pain, however, because they never said a word about it, sort of a reverse of what I had experienced as a child when I was left behind. I was just as guilty of being insensitive to them - no feelings for anyone else except myself. This promotion and path is what I had been waiting for, dreaming for.
Ready, set, go –

Off we went in January full of dreams, confidence and excitement in ourselves and the good things happening to us. We were on our way.

Again, I was the one writing the notes to my own song in all my self-confidence, while the crickets sang away in Wisconsin. I didn't hear them.

We bought a new house, met the neighbors, made some new friends and joined a Bible study. Life was good – but cold in Wisconsin. There was no such thing as snow days because the snow plows just barreled through with the cars on the road and all. I felt like we were living on top of the Earth; it seemed like a long way from our home in Ohio. Wisconsin was beautiful, and I was not homesick but felt free and safe with my little family. There were lots of cute chalet-looking shops. Lake Michigan was nearby with a little zoo in the area and my little family rode our bikes to lots of neat places near our house to feed the Canadian Geese.

We were very excited about Jeff's new job and his early promotion; everything seemed to be the way it was supposed to be – the American dream was really happening to Jeff and Gail.

We worked on our house and covered the lawn with sod. We were just having a great time exploring the area.

We were there nine months.

Then it happened – one night after work, Jeff shuffled in the door announcing that he was being laid-off.

What!

"Laid-off, what does that mean?"

The company was experiencing a downturn, and a few people from his department were being let go.

DEVASTATION!

DARKNESS!

PANIC!

UNBELIEF!

SHOCK!

What were we to do?

How would we pay our bills?

Who would help us?

We had six weeks to find a new job!

Six weeks!!

Six weeks!!!

Six weeks!!!!

Six weeks!!!!!

Help!!!!!!

I prayed desperately.

In shock and torment, we immediately buckled Keri in her car seat, plopped in the car and drove down to my brother's house in Chicago. Surely, he would help us understand - counsel us -and know what to do. My brother comforted us as best as he could. No one could figure out why we had no warning, why they would move us all the way up there, pay those relocation expenses to just dump us and dumped is exactly how I felt. How could this be? This wasn't supposed to happen.

I was deaf to any crickets singing that night. No music, no peace, no security. I just felt panic and darkness and very bad for Jeff. But God was there and the crickets were singing for me while He kept writing my song.

"Call a recruiter," someone suggested.

Jeff began the stress-filled adventure of looking for a new job and trying to regain his confidence after this jolt. The next day, he picked up the phone and called a recruiter. The recruiter was encouraging.

"Don't worry. This happens all the time."

It does! I didn't know this. That was very unsettling. Whatever happened to our American dream?

Spiritual training had begun. God in His mercy and faithfulness created two job offers in six weeks on Jeff's last day at his company – one in our town in Wisconsin and one back home in Ohio.

WOW!

WHEW!

That was scary!

That was cool!

What a relief!

Thank you so much, God.

I knew God had taken care of us. There was no doubt in my mind. This was no accident, but a genuine miracle as far as I was concerned. Now, our prayer had been answered, and we were rescued. Now, I could relax with our new job. Now, we would get our American dream back in motion and be on our way. God had rescued us and, now, things would be OK. This was just a momentary:

glitch

interruption

bad dream

annoyance

fluke

The threatening crisis was over - quick. We knew we wanted to move back to Ohio, to Marion. I was very excited about the move:

closer to home

warmer weather
earlier spring
a new house
a new job
a new dream

Ready, set, go –

again, but with not so much confidence in ourselves this time. A broken place had been created, a small doubt, a little dependency. We survived the ordeal very well - no post-traumatic stress syndrome or anything like that, and we were expecting wonderful success back in Ohio. We went to Marion and our new job, feeling very happy and carrying all our naive perceptions of life with us.

We had been blessed and another note had been added to my song.

Little did I know what was ahead, and that God was going to use Marion, Ohio to open my spiritual eyes.

Chapter 9

Chicken Noodle Soup

> Do not conform any longer to the pattern of this world, but be transformed by the renewing of your mind.... Romans 12:2

Did you know that the crickets make melody of God's love in Marion, Ohio? I didn't. But they do, and they were there – loud and clear.

Marion, Ohio was the place where God opened my spiritual eyes in a huge way.

We had just been rescued from a threat:

a job loss

bills to pay

a dreadful situation

scary

dark

hurtful

upsetting

We had experienced a miracle – a deliverance at the last minute.

God Didn't Have to Make the Crickets Sing

Now we needed a new home. Jeff had received a small raise in salary, and I knew exactly the kind of house I wanted - dreamed about - the typical two-story home with the family room behind the garage. I really wanted a fireplace this time and two bathrooms. I would know it when I saw it. I said a simple prayer and began looking.

We found a development that we both liked. My faith in God for house-hunting was pretty meager at that time; I just knew that God had saved us from devastation and that we were moving forward.

We found a split-level at the end of a street. It was really the only one that looked available in that area, but it was not really what I wanted. It had a different floor plan, and I was feeling somewhat disappointed.

We were staying with my parents a few days while we looked for a house. My sister, Ann, was visiting my folks while we were planning our move. I began sharing my disappointment about the house that we found.

"Maybe you haven't found your house yet," she said after we got home from looking that day. I heard her but really didn't pay much attention.

We drove back to Marion the next day planning to buy that split-level. We stopped in the realtor's office to close the deal. It was "OK" - I guess; we needed a place to live, and I liked the area.

Jeff sat at the realtor's desk flipping through the multiple-listings book as we all talked about that spilt-level. He stopped turning the pages. "What about this house?"

"Oh, that house just finished its listing, but I think it is still available."

It was THE house – in the same neighborhood! There it was – that was it – perfect:
two-story
family room behind the garage
fireplace

two bathrooms
colonial
perfect, just like I wanted

I couldn't believe it! God did this – He knew my wishes, my heart - personal. And again, it was at the last minute. He had brought us completely through our ordeal and had met every need and more. The whole thing was under His control:

unbelievable!
wonderful!
amazing!
stupendous!
incredible!
exactly the house at the last minute!
Thank you so much, God!

A complete rescue - a blessing and provision from His hand. **But, believe it or not, I still didn't hear any crickets.**

Now, God had helped us; we probably would be OK - probably not need His help for a long time. We would take over from here. Now, we had our job and our house. Now, we would see our dreams come true.

He had answered my prayers and quickly. I saw God as my Rescuer, Helper and Problem-solver but not as a Person so intimately involved with me every day that He could meet all my emotional needs. He was still on the outside. I needed to know Him on the inside. I thought that my needs were still being met in:

my husband
my children
my home
Jeff's job
the good life
my dreams

We moved in right before Christmas, and I met the neighbors, nice, friendly, corporate wives. We talked and visited, played tennis and went shopping, had lunch and enjoyed normal conversation. Life was like it was supposed to be for me, like when I grew up. Yet, I knew that I had just experienced an amazing miracle - a provision from God - and had been saved from grave danger. I really wanted to share this story with everyone! This was my life story right now, but my mouth was still shut.

Life was good for us in Marion - very good. It was a place where we were very happy and enjoyed almost five years of the good life:

having two more children
Christian friends
tennis leagues
promotions for Jeff
a Master's degree in accounting for Jeff from Ashland University
becoming a decent amateur oil painter and winning 1st place at the local county fair
riding bikes with our kids around the block
playing hide-and-go-seek in the house
having our parents up for holidays
going to visit them sometimes on the weekends
swimming

My fondest family memories were there because we were still enjoying the innocence of life and our young children. Our circumstances were cooperating and comfortable.

And I was starting to experience some prayer answers:

We lost our car keys at a company picnic. As we prayed and looked around a small park, Keri's friend dropped her sunglasses on the grass. The keys were right beside the glasses in the grass.

I discovered a new Christian contemporary radio station.

I relaxed after a misdiagnosis of my newborn son while we were still in the hospital. It turned out to be that of another baby; "We are so sorry; this just never happens," said the nurse. "The doctors always check the babies before they talk to the moms."

We found a necklace that I had put in Keri's lunch sack on the first day of school in the school dumpster filled with trashed lunch bags. She didn't know the necklace was in her sack and had thrown it away after lunch. As we checked the dumpster after school, we opened one of several large trash bags and found Keri's necklace in the first trashed lunch bag that we opened.

I just kept living my life, thinking about and so impressed with the rescue we had just experienced from Wisconsin. I felt closer to God than ever. But I was still silent.

Crickets were singing away all around the house, and God was adding several more notes to my melody.

One day, out of the blue, a thought popped into my head as I was walking across the back yard -

"People can't see Me. You sound like everyone else."

It was true, and I knew it. The answer from this past crisis had made a deep impression on me. It stuck. When I talked to my friends, I *did* sound like everyone else talking about common life with all the gossip and complaining. But I wanted to be free of it. I deeply wanted to share my blessing that I had just experienced about my wonderful God. But I had no power to share my faith.

Another day, I was upstairs washing a bedroom window. I was still struggling with unrealistic expectations from my marriage and past hurts. "Where did the love go? Where are all the warm feelings? I don't feel connected like I did in Washington?" Something was still missing, and I was still looking in all the wrong places for satisfaction. I could get no satisfaction. Oh, I loved and enjoyed my husband, but there were still those occasional arguments about ballgames.

Then another thought -

"You deal with life through anger."

Again, I knew it had to be the Holy Spirit, and it was true. I did bark at Jeff too much.

But everyday life went on – those two impressions stuck but produced no real change in me.

And then, one night - it happened.

Jeff had decided to have nasal surgery. For years, he had trouble breathing because he broke his nose in high school playing basketball. After the surgery, his nose was packed up pretty tight, and it was very swollen and very painful. He was sitting at our kitchen table complaining about the pain. Because of my poor attitude and emotional scars - fantasies from the past about relationships - I wasn't very sympathetic. After all, I worked hard too - being there for him and taking care of him - where was my hug?

That evening, I was stirring some chicken noodle soup that I had made for him when I became aware of two thoughts in my head -

"Aren't you tired of hearing him complain?" one thought blared.

"I know every diaper that you change. Is that enough?" the other thought whispered.

This was different, more impressions and two thoughts - a spiritual battle, a choice - in my head.

I had to choose, and I knew which thought was right. I knew which thought was from God. Who else would say that? He knew everything I did. In fact, I realized, all of a sudden, that everything I did was for Him, not for Jeff or for anyone else.

I was:

cleaning the house for Him
making casseroles for Him
sweeping the rugs for Him
washing clothes for Him
fixing lunches for Him
sewing for Him
taking care of my family for Him

He was my Boss, my accountability factor, and He noticed and He cared. My service was to Him, and my reward would come from Him. My focus and contentment was to be in Him,

not in the people I was living with. I could give and receive from Him. The experience was:
- intimate
- immediate
- powerful
- eye-opening
- a realization that I really was not alone

This was so *huge* for me, and I was set free. Almost instantly, I was freed from my negative emotions, my negative reactions of those around me - my fantasies, my emotional demands - because I realized that I wasn't pleasing man, I was pleasing God. Yes, He did know every diaper that I changed, and it was enough, more than enough. *He* was enough, and I had found my need in Him. For me, a light bulb went off – a true awareness of the spiritual. Right away, I knew that I had been born-again so many years ago. The spiritual world came alive - very alive. Something had really happened to me when I was fourteen, when I became a believer at that slumber party. I had been born of a spiritual seed inside of me - the Holy Spirit, so:
- real
- delicate
- powerful
- thoughtful

Temptations of good and evil thoughts were in my head, and I could choose which one to listen to. I had been born-again, and the people who didn't know Christ didn't have a clue about this spiritual life - they were blinded. They didn't see it or get it. They didn't understand the spiritual - their thought life, their bondage. They couldn't choose; they couldn't even catch the thoughts to make a choice. They:
- were spiritually dead
- were out of relationship with God
- were cut off by their sin
- were lost

were in darkness
were unenlightened
needed the Savior
needed to be born- again

The Lord Jesus Christ had come alive to me in my inner man. How powerful:

my new birth
my new awareness
my new thoughts
renewing my mind
how compelling

I began to devour the book of Romans and the epistles. As I became aware of my spiritual life and renewed my mind in His word, I could control my emotions by my thoughts from God's promises to me - find inner peace, strength and purpose each day, each moment.

I began receiving a magazine called *Fullness* in the mail every month. To this day, I don't know how I got it, but it had powerful articles about:

Christ in you
spiritual warfare
faith
the new birth
our enemy
prayer

I consumed it page by page each month and still have them saved in my house. I couldn't get enough of this new awareness. God and the spiritual world were real to me – now - and I had experienced the spiritual reality that occurred from my prayer at 14.

I began writing small poems:
Jesus lives inside of me
I know now this is so.
I used to believe it in my head,

But now I know, I know.
I love Him like I love no one
He's fabulous, faithful and true.
I love what's happening inside of me
I'm changing, becoming anew.

A friend, Marianne, from our church, was experiencing the same spiritual awakening at just about the same time that I was. She was reading Watchman Nee's book *The Normal Christian Life* and outlining it. I got a copy and read through it. It was deep and hard to understand – about the old Adam, the new Adam and our flesh being dead - a study of Romans. But I kept rereading it, at least three times, and the spiritual truths about renewing your mind began making sense. The spiritual world had opened up, and I saw it brighter and clearer. The Bible made more sense to me - now.

I tried to explain to Jeff what had happened to me - how exciting it was to renew our minds in the truth of God's word and watch out for the tempting thoughts. I told him how real the spiritual world was, how practical the Bible was for overcoming negative emotions and that God was really there. He didn't seem to get it or be too interested.

During this time, I was asked to teach the high school Sunday school class at our church since the former teacher had quit. I began putting studies together about spiritual warfare, the new man, renewing your mind and temptation. The high school attendance began to increase.

One parent told me, "I don't know what you are teaching in your class, but my son loves to come. He actually gets up in the morning and looks forward to coming."

I agreed. This new awareness from the Bible was so powerful - exciting - and should be proclaimed.

Soon after that, I discovered a breast lump one evening around 11:00 while I was sitting on the couch watching a late night program.

"You better get that toy for Kelly that you saw at the store because you are going to be dead by Christmas," whispered the enemy as the thought penetrated my head.

Because of my spiritual armor and awareness, I immediately dismissed the thought, gave myself to God and went to bed. I knew that God was taking care of me, and I decided:

not to talk about it

not feel it every moment

to go to the doctor

to keep my focus on the Lord

And it worked - I maintained a powerful peace and strength.

I made an appointment with the doctor. "Oh, that's just a small, common fibroid tumor."

"Well, I still want it removed," I said.

I had saved myself hours of fear, tears and scary dialogue as I kept quiet, took the problem to the doctor and kept my focus on the Lord. I went through outpatient surgery - calm and alert.

"Wow, you seem to have a lot of peace," said the nurse. I told her that I knew the Lord Jesus.

I did have peace. I had learned a wonderful strategy during this spiritual warfare – *keep my focus on the Lord* - something I knew unsaved people know nothing about, and it worked to keep me in peace. My life belonged to God, and I was so excited about what I had discovered. The Holy Spirit was really in me. I could feel the strength, and I trusted God's word – stood on it – renewing my mind.

Life went on, and I continued to grow and learn those amazing spiritual principles from scripture. Being a Christian is not about death, but about our new life - here.

We were in Marion almost five years. Jeff worked for a company that made large coal shovels. With the souring energy economy, the company was losing sales. Slowly, the downsizing creature showed his ugly face again. We survived many layoffs, but finally the "death angel" gave Jeff his pink slip along with many others. The company became a skeleton of what it had been.

Jeff had finished his Master's degree, and we were very excited about the future, the new opportunities that God surely would open up for us. We were completely excited and very confident. After all, Jeff had done it right again:

Master's Degree
seven years' experience in accounting
ambitious
great personality

What a resume, what a catch - an asset to any company. And I knew that we had God with us this time. Our expectancy was in Him. I had seen it, knew Him, watched Him take care of us from the get go. I knew He must have a great plan for us - that great job and life that we had so believed we were all about.

Our son, Dan, had just been born, and Jeff and I enjoyed being together with our little family for the majority of his first year while Jeff looked for a job. It was all very exciting, and I was full of faith.

But, again, God had a different set of plans in mind to form me into the image of His Son – to develop:

faith
trust
character
perseverance
spiritual life
dependency
power

Lurking in the distance was a monster. I didn't know its name. It was a deadly beast who would try to destroy our lives, and I didn't see it hiding in the shadows - coming around the corner. God in His mercy didn't let me see it coming. This terrifying monster would deeply test my relationship to God to the extreme - my faith and my surrender.

God Didn't Have to Make the Crickets Sing

The crickets were still singing along the way, but the song of security and peace was still outside and not in my deepest soul.

God still had some work to do

Chapter 10

The American Dream

"... Never will I leave you; never will I forsake you." Hebrews 13:5

We had been out of work for eight months. Because of the poor economy in the early 80's, our unemployment had been extended, but it was going to run out at the end of the year in December. Jeff had been busy interviewing. It was all very exciting to us.

We were claiming God's promise that, "He will give you the desires of your heart." That is what the Bible said, and my faith was very strong. After all, hadn't we seen God deliver us quite a few times before? We knew He was there and with us. Both of us believed that. We were just claiming scripture for our plan, our desires. We were almost too cocky and not broken.

We thought we wanted to go and settle in Virginia. We loved that state, bustling and beautiful with its rolling hills, a great place to raise a family. I just knew God was going to do this – give us our hearts' desire. We were totally trusting in Him; He was going to come through again with *our* plan.

God Didn't Have to Make the Crickets Sing

Around late October with about two months of unemployment left, a recruiter called.

"I've got three possibilities with a Fortune 100 pharmaceutical company. One of the positions is in Michigan, one is in Columbus and one is in Virginia. Are you interested?"

"Yes, oh, yes!" This had to be it - Virginia!

"Isn't it neat to see ahead of time what God is doing?" I retorted rather flippantly to Jeff. I didn't feel flippant - just confident - because, after all, we knew our God. We were growing closer to Him and also to the end of our unemployment checks coming in. The timing was right – the last minute. I had learned that. But we were going to be rescued again and, this time, off to Virginia. He wouldn't fail us. We had faith, and we were claiming it.

Well, the recruiter called back to tell us the job in Michigan was filled. Whew! I didn't want to go there anyway. But then another call came, and God closed the door to Virginia as well. Oh, well! Jeff was to interview in Columbus which was still a great opportunity for us – a desirable, alternative location to our dream state, and we needed a job - and we needed it quick! Jeff got a second interview in Columbus and then a third and our hopes were high.

But in a few days, we watched that opportunity go south.

Now, the pressure and the worry began tempting us. It was approaching Thanksgiving, and we had no real possibilities. The phone wasn't ringing, and the old worries surfaced:

We need a job - soon.

What would we do with no unemployment checks?

How would we pay our bills?

We were totally vulnerable.

The worry and pressure was on – and growing. We traveled to Chicago to have Thanksgiving with my brother's family and my parents. We were both pretty down, concerned and scared. We could *see* no hope out there.

"How's the job search going?" everyone asked, concerned.

I tried to hide my anxiety, "Oh, fine, God's going to take care of us." I got the words out ever so bravely - feebly - shaking in my shoes, trying to sound like a victorious Christian.

But inside, I was beginning to feel worried and fearful. The desire of our hearts seemed to be dying. I clung to just a weak hope in the Bible promise:

"And my God will meet all your needs according to his glorious riches in Christ Jesus." Philippians 4:19

God was adding more notes to the stanzas while I was holding, clutching, grasping onto that promise with all my might. I had no deep assurance and heard no cricket song.

We came back from Chicago feeling pretty worried.

Around the middle of December, Jeff got a call from a personnel director; another Fortune 100 company had responded favorably to Jeff's resume, and they wanted an interview. Off he went. They liked him so much, they offered him the job on the spot – two weeks before the unemployment ran out!

WHEW! - dodged that bullet again!

We had seen this before but were hanging on for dear life when the job finally came. I still had no sense:

of security
of sovereignty
of safety
of confidence
of power
of peace
in this God – this God of my salvation

I carried just a weak hope in a Bible promise that He would meet my needs.

Needless to say, we were both very, very relieved. The economy in Marion was tanking in the early 80's with at least five big companies closing or downsizing. Every day we looked down our street and saw five houses for sale. We would have been left high-and-dry if the unemployment checks had stopped.

Well, thank you, God, and we were excited! We were moving to Indiana. It was all very appealing to both of us:

midsized town
good restaurants
Fortune 100 company
a new beginning
a step up
the American dream
great schools
great neighborhood

And they even had a large mall! I was certainly happy about that.

Ready, set, go –

We moved onto Jamestown Road in Colonial park. The street beside us was named Williamsburg Lane. The first new neighbors that we met were both from Virginia! We also were greeted by another neighbor who lived around the corner and, you guessed it, had moved to Indiana from Virginia. This was a hoot and just too much.

Was this a personal God trying to tell us He knew us and our desires?

Jeff had received another raise, and we bought a lovely colonial home that he had picked out for us. We bought it on a land contract from the owners since our house in Marion had not sold yet. Jeff's work was down the street, a stone's throw from our house. The addition was out in a lovely, newly developed area.

Whoa! For me, this was quite an answer – *the* answer. We had arrived. Here it was - the house, the job and the neighborhood - the American dream realized. God had done it - really done it this time, and I was so very impressed and thankful. I can't say enough about how awesome I felt about my God - I was literally on fire for Him! He was really with us and had saved us again. And now, I really didn't sound like everyone else.

I wanted to tell everyone that:

I was a Christian.

I knew God.

Dreams do come true.

God had been so good.

He was faithful.

They could be saved.

But my relationship with God was still in prayer answers, Bible verses and Bible studies, not in reaching my deepest soul and the needs that were there – my security and peace - my rest. I hadn't been broken yet. I was still strong in myself – in the world - in what it said to do.

We found a wonderful church and met many great people, lots of corporate wives moving around with their husbands, all chasing the American dream. They were stay-at-home moms raising their children with husbands in management.

I witnessed discreetly to some of my new friends and found out my next door neighbor was a Christian. I made friends with another dear mom who lived down the street. She eventually prayed to receive Christ as her Savior in my living room. This was all just wonderful; it confirmed to me that we were in the right place. It was what I was about – sharing how to know this wonderful God who had taken such good care of us.

I began settling in – really settling in this time - and decorating my house. I dug my emotional roots deep in Indiana. This was going to be our home, our life and our promise, and it felt so right. I settled in to stay. The company was stable, and it looked like we would not be transferred anywhere anytime soon. This *was* our home, and we both loved it.

Jeff enjoyed his new job and worked closely with his boss. The boss was grooming him to take a job that another retiring employee would soon leave open, the job Jeff had been really hired for:

a job with more responsibility

a job with more pay

a job he was more qualified for

a job that had been promised

a job up the next step of the corporate ladder

Jeff was overqualified for the job that he took and looked forward to eventually making this change with a promotion. There were many promises made to us, and we believed them all hook, line and sinker.

We began living our dream:

Jeff went to work every day.

I took care of the kids every day.

We enjoyed our family every day.

We got a dog.

We joined a tennis league in the summer.

We got involved in our church every Sunday.

We had neighborhood garage sales every Mother's Day.

We went caroling at Christmas.

But there was one slight problem – our house in Marion still hadn't sold. It had been one year, and I couldn't understand why God was delaying this for us.

My father, the banker, said, "You're going to have trouble selling your house in this economy."

But I knew God was with us in this and didn't pay much attention to his words.

But it still took two years to sell our house. God was very faithful and supplied renters back in Ohio during that time. We actually made money on the deal and had a realtor watching over our house and still trying to sell it. But I still couldn't understand why God wasn't completing this venture and selling our house for us so we could move on.

After one year passed, Jeff said, "I'm going to the bank and see if we can go ahead and buy the house. We have the down payment."

"Good idea," I thought. "Let's get this done."

He came back from the bank and said, "The bank won't loan us the money. They don't want to take the risk until I get a raise because we haven't sold our house in Marion."

Oh, that's cool. We're living in a house that we can't afford. But Jeff had been promised a nice promotion any day. I just wasn't concern. I knew we were supposed to be there because I had met a dear friend who had prayed to receive the Savior on my couch in my living room. She was impacting others in a mighty way. Also, the whole Virginia thing was weird. But I still couldn't figure it out.

Another year later, Jeff got a raise in December. That very same month, we sold our old house in Marion. The raise meant we were making enough money now, and we secured our loan and bought our new house.

Whoa! Thank you, God - right on time, again. There was a plan and again God proved Himself:

faithful

beyond belief

amazing

secure

personal

What did you ever have to worry about, Gail? Relax! Relax! This faith, God-thing, was just too cool.

My mom moved to a retirement home near us after my father died. Our life had settled in – *really* settled in, and we were very happy building our future.

I was trusting God for the external stuff - to make our dream job, dream life come true. Oh, I watched for the rapture, witnessed to friends, went to church and prayed, but it was still all about thanking God for His answers and going on my merry way expecting this blessing He provided to last a long time - very external.

My security was in these companies. That was all I knew. I knew about spiritual warfare with thoughts and emotions. I knew nothing about:

walking in the Spirit
being broken
being dependent
intimacy with Christ
the song

Who wanted to be broken and go through something dark, hard and scary - anyway? Not me, buddy! I wasn't there yet. I did not understand that God was Sovereign in our lives and in control. He was daily transforming us, working with us and guiding us. It was not about the jobs, but it was about us and our walk with Him, our peace and joy, our patience and meekness – a path to lead us into a deeper awareness that He *really* was there – molding us, shaping us.

His path was about developing:
faith
love
humility
spiritual growth
dependence on Him
spiritual power
character

Dependence was not a word I knew or even liked. I was very independent and full of life, but still needy inside and still that little insecure girl who grew up with babysitters - still believing that close family and the good life was the meaning to life and still looking to husbands, jobs and family to do it for me.

God was there to get me out of a jam, witness for Him and wait for His return and not much more. When the answer to a problem would come, *I* would take it, and *I* would do it - thank you. He was not my life or breath. I had self-confidence, not God-confidence, to live my life.

I just figured that God had made the crickets, and they knew how to chirp. It meant nothing to me personally, no song for me.

Life looked real good, and I was determined to have it. This is what I had been taught:

go to college

work hard

succeed

go up the ladder

move around with your husband

the American dream

However, a monster was beginning to move - rapidly approaching with impending dark and dangerous - devastating fangs.

I often wondered about people who had been radically saved. I was a good girl, from an average middle-class family. I had parents and family who loved me and some friends. But I had heard those powerful testimonies of people who found Christ in crisis with a profound change in their lives. That was not mine. I didn't have a radically saved experience at that slumber party when I was 14. I knew there had been a change – could feel it deep inside. God said I needed saved, and I believed Him. I knew that I had sinned, and I prayed. My life was changed, but I didn't experience the inner presence that some seemed to talk about.

I didn't come from:

a broken family

drugs

promiscuity

jail

being a single parent

abuse

addiction

divorce

What would that be like to be so broken and meet Jesus? How would that feel? Would there be a powerful experience – a sense of His presence? I wondered. I just didn't know. However, one day in the future, I would find out.

Chapter 11

The Monster

"When I am afraid, I will trust in you." Psalm 56:3

It had been three years with the company, and the job Jeff had been consistently groomed for – promised, hired for - was not opening up. This became a source of frustration for him and created some friction between us as I tried to encourage him to trust God. He didn't get it yet - spiritual warfare. Why didn't he trust God for this? It was uncomfortable and was putting some pressure between us. I was enjoying a great life:

my husband
my kids
my dog
my friends
my tennis
my church
my house
sharing Christ
caring for my mom

God Didn't Have to Make the Crickets Sing

My close Christian friend and I began praying everyday about this promotion that Jeff had been promised and some serious financial needs that she had.

One day – a thought – a bewildering thought:

"I'm going to use Jeff's job in his spiritual life." It happened in my kitchen again. I wrote it down on a notepad and tucked it away next to some cookbooks, not giving it much attention.

What did that mean? I knew he needed to grow spiritually, we all did. My experience with God had been confronting a crisis, praying madly and God rescuing us to say, "Whew, thank you, God. Now we can enjoy the answer, the job and the good life."

I had no idea how deeply God could write the notes in my heart so that I could hear the crickets' song someday.

I kept praying for Jeff. We didn't seem to be on the same page spiritually – maybe, we never were. Was he even saved?

Suddenly, the vicious monster attacked.

One day after work, Jeff came through our front door badly shaken with news. The job he had been promised had opened up. His boss had contacted management so that he could offer it to Jeff. He came back and said, "I guess you have to interview for the job."

Then, in a couple of weeks, the news - the disturbing news, it had been given to someone else – a woman, an international.

For us and our dreams, it was devastating and defeating. We just didn't understand. It was a known fact that Jeff was being groomed for this job, was hired for this job and was promised this job. This job was everything we wanted, our future, our step up, and we had been denied - he had been denied - betrayed. My soul was emptied, feeling my husband's great:

pain
hurt
loss
disappointment

darkness

anger

There was a gaping hole in my stomach.

The name of the monster was "affirmative action," and it had snuck in our door with a vengeance hitting us - big time - with the politics of corporate America. Corporate America had been pretty good to us so far, but now we had been betrayed – a cherished promise broken and our future shattered as we saw it. Where was the loyalty, the commitment? This was so unfair and such a breach of trust. A monstrous system had turned around and bit us - bit us hard - in our deepest soul. How could this happen?

What do you do when something like this hits you? You fall apart - at least I did. My light had turned to darkness. I wasn't raised in a family of faith. I didn't know about walking in the Spirit – that God was Sovereign in our lives and had a path - a crooked path. We were both so naïve to the ways of the world, so trusting - so honest. We were not prepared for this - at all, especially my husband who was a great employee, hard-working, innocent and full of dreams.

Needless to say, after this disappointing chaos, his work environment became more stressful and threatening for him. Before this ordeal, Jeff could do no wrong; now little mistakes became bigger issues. It became more and more uncomfortable. There had been a breach of trust. The department seemed to be turning on him.

What do you say to your boss after the company has betrayed you and he is caught in the middle? Jeff and his boss had collaborated, cooperated and planned on this promotion for Jeff for nearly three years. It seemed like that was all they talked about. How do you work with fellow employees in the department who feel terrible for you? Everyone loved Jeff and was looking forward to him taking over. After a few weeks, it became obvious to us that we needed to move on and look for another job.

But, the darkness, the hopelessness:
But where?
But when?
But how?
But what about our kids?
But what about their school?
But what about all our friends?
But what about our dog?
But what about my mom? I couldn't worry her with this. What would happen to her?

I had been emptied, destroyed deep inside – no confidence, no dream and no hope any more. It was all very, very, very dark!

Starting over was unthinkable at that time for both or us – our confidence was crushed - shattered. We were just so broken. We didn't want to leave our dream, our home and go somewhere else. It was supposed to be here.

During the summer - late at night - after everyone had gone to bed while the crickets were singing their lovely music all around my front porch, all I heard were my tears, sobs, desperate prayers frantically praying - begging - God to help us as I sat there night after night.

I sat on my porch before I went to bed every night looking up at the stars. Everyone else was sleeping. I didn't really know what to pray, but I was in so much fear, pain and darkness. I couldn't see anything ahead – total blindness. I had no strength to do this. God just kept on working, writing my notes, waiting - waiting for me to hear - breaking my flesh and my self-reliance - sometimes violently, sometimes slowly and silently, methodically, securely.

I called my beloved pastor, and he was wonderful.
"This is just politics."
I thought;
"No, this is just mean."

"This is cruel."
"This is evil."
"This is unnecessary."
"This is over-the-top."
"This is wrong."
"This is a broken promise."

He was extremely sympathetic about our situation. But one day he told me, "Gail, you need to go through this to see what life can really be like for others if you are ever going to have genuine compassion for people" – God's compassion.

He was right. I grew up privileged - clueless and unaware of the deep pain that some carry through life. My struggles back then seemed minor compared to this darkness.

The steps in the dark began – blind steps –foggy, painful steps going nowhere. How does a person recover from something like this? It was terrible, beyond anything I had ever experienced. My life had been full of ambition, hope, education and dreams – not this, and we had reached them – here. Now they were being taken away, torn away. I couldn't control my life now; I was totally helpless. It wasn't exciting anymore.

Now, I was on a new, threatening adventure – God's adventure – His plan, not mine anymore. He had allowed a deep cut, and it felt:

insecure
unsettling
scary
vulnerable
hopeless
painful

But it really wasn't because I was in His hands – God's hands; He had gone beyond the external and was now digging into the internal. He was messing with my soul – my inner man - killing the confidence of my flesh and strengthening the spirit.

Jeff began interviewing. I struggled in absolute fear as I watched him try to deal with the destructive, negative emotions - stress and anger - he was feeling and the thoughts playing over and over in his head about how this could have happened and how decent people could do such a thing.

The dream had evaporated – our American dream was gone.

The monster greeted me each morning when I opened my eyes. I asked God to keep Satan and his negative attacks away from my bed first thing in the morning. I told myself, "I know I will be somewhere five years from now, but where, how?" I was so vulnerable, not in control emotionally. It felt strange, threatening and very uncomfortable. I tied a rope around my soul, attached the end to God and His word and hung on for dear life. I consumed the Psalms.

God seemed silent except for His word. I hung on to any encouragement I heard – hung onto our pastor's words almost everyday:

This will work out.

God is there.

Keep your focus on Him.

Hang on to His promises in the Bible.

Pray.

My only security that I knew had been threatened:

my husband

his career

our dream

our future

my faith

This was hard - really hard - and very painful for my husband, hard to care, hard to dream again and to be ready to go after something like this. Disillusionment, devastation - no dreams now - just one gigantic, big, black nightmare tormented me throughout the day. And I had to dig deep - very deep - to keep going.

But God had not left us at all. My true security, Father, Boss, Guide and Hope was still there – always there:

spurring us on

beckoning to our souls to look to Him

comforting us

creating a new dream

holding our hands

taking charge again

This was impossible for me. He would eventually have to put all my pieces back together. He went to work immediately, and I would be dragged away from my cherished dream in Indiana. Would I ever feel normal again?

"... And surely I am with you always, to the very end of the age." Matthew 28:20

Chapter 12

Green Pastures

> The Lord is my Shepherd, I shall not be in want. He makes me lie down in green pastures, He leads me beside quiet waters, He restores my soul.... Psalm 23:1-2

I was a mess; my emotions had overtaken my faith - my mustard-sized faith, and I really hadn't learned that God was enough:

my security

my stability

I lay on my bed at night wondering where in the world we were going and what it would be like. I had lost control of my life – completely, and it terrified me. I never wanted this to happen to me again - ever.

"Eight is the number of new beginnings. Maybe you'll get your job in the eight month," said my older born-again sister as I called her for prayer almost every night in sheer panic – crying and sharing my pain. She was my encourager, a faithful encourager; she was my strength. I just didn't have my own strength in God - yet.

As our broken path continued, Jeff was offered a job back in Ohio – Greenville. I thought that the place sounded like those green pastures that it talks about in the Psalms. It was another Fortune 500 company with a sweet, young, unintimidating Christian boss. This had promise – looked like a place to heal. But the town was so small - so tiny – not someplace that looked at all reasonable or desirable to me; I certainly had no wish to leave my home and move to that little town. Did it even have a mall?

God silently kept adding more notes to my future lovely chorus.

We reluctantly put our house up for sale. We sold our house in two weeks!

I went to the small town to look for a new house with Helen, the realtor. She was so sweet and took me around to see what we could find. My heart was still back in Indiana where I loved my old home, but I had learned that I could trust God with this need of finding a house.

I had no worry, but was very numb about the whole thing. I called my pastor back in Indiana and told him, "I don't know if I can do this."

"You have no choice!" was his stark, commanding reply. I just had to do this difficult thing. After all, I had:

a husband to encourage

children to raise

a home to establish in a brand new place

and myself to heal emotionally

The realtor and I drove around the tiny town. I only found one house that looked like a slim possibility. As we continued driving and looking, I spotted a house that I liked very much, but it wasn't for sale.

"I really want a house like that. How much would that house cost?"

She quoted me a price that we could afford.

"Gee, I wish that house was for sale," I said.

God Didn't Have to Make the Crickets Sing

I went back to Indiana while Jeff moved to Greenville to begin his new job. He continued to look for houses with the realtor.

Then it happened – a phone call one evening when I was wrapping Christmas presents. It was Jeff.

"Hey, there is a new house on the market, and I know you would really like it."

As he described it, I knew it was THAT HOUSE. I loved that house.

In guarded excitement, I asked, "How much is it?"

When he told me the price, it was $15,000 more than we could afford.

"That's nice, but it costs too much," I sighed giving up.

We chatted a minute or two, and then I went back to wrapping my Christmas presents.

Then – a new thought:

"This is my Christmas present to you."

What did that mean? Was that really you, God?

After we sold our house and prepared to move, Jeff had located a nice large duplex on the outskirts of town near the elementary school. We gave our dog, Lady, to our favorite babysitter who adored her.

The moving van came the day after Christmas. We packed up and God pulled me out of Indiana.

Ready. . . . . set. . . . . go. . . . . in a tremendously numb and distorted way.

There were:

no dreams

no feelings of confidence

many unanswered questions

many emotional wounds

many fears

I was walking blindly, following a path – God's path along God's school of brokenness.

We were both pretty shaken, and I was following in meager faith. This was different this time, a leading of God that did not seem exciting at all but hurtful, debilitating, threatening, and, yet, the same God who had rescued us before was still working. It just didn't feel good this time. My meager strength was beginning to come from Him – but that didn't give me peace. I was hanging on for dear life.

The duplex was located in a quiet, isolated place on the outskirts of town, a place for me to heal:

peaceful, green country
the elementary school right down the street
no neighbors
solitude
a little country church right down the street
a beautiful small pond behind our duplex
winter

As we settled in, the crickets would soon sing again as they prepared their song through the winter.

It was the green pasture I needed. I was guarded, hurt and dazed. I didn't want to meet anyone. I needed time to unwind my tangled emotions and land on my feet. I didn't want to talk about anything. No questions like:

Where did you guys move from?
What does your husband do?
Where do you live?
What do you like to do?

Nothing, absolutely nothing – just support Jeff in his new job, get the kids acclimated to their new school and enjoy being with my young 4-year old son, Danny. It worked and for four months I relaxed with my family and kept my eye on that house.

One day after we moved into the duplex, our realtor called, "The house you were asking about is being bought by a holding company which means the price will probably go down."

Great, wonderful – but $15,000.00! No way.

But the Christmas thought said "This is my Christmas present to you," and I really liked that house very much:
two-story cedar-sided house
beautiful family room and fireplace
french doors to the deck
railing along the upstairs hall
newly redecorated in all my colors
beautiful bay window with shutters in the eating area
deck
nice, open back yard with a wonderful weeping willow tree
four nice, large bedrooms
nicely landscaped
a home

I really liked it better than our old house in Indiana. I dared to hope and dream again that maybe this *would* work out. I wanted that to happen for us, and it helped draw me into my new surroundings.

By April, no one had bid on the house. They sold it to us for $15,000.00 less than the original asking price!

Again, amazing!

Again, wonderful!

Again, God reveals Himself!

Again, I see Him with us!

Again, He knocks my socks off!

More notes.

What a wonderful impression this made on my children and me – to pick out a house before it was even for sale and watch it come down $15,000.00! To this day, it is one of God's loving and powerful answers to me when I was so broken. It left a huge impression – a huge memory and a huge reminder of His grace and care of me every day - every second.

In April, we moved into our new house.

In time, we adjusted nicely to our new home. I enjoyed the house very much and the town. It was small, but friendly and quaint. We could ride our bikes to the high school tennis courts, the neighborhood park and the swimming pool. I made one good friend with a wife of a fellow employee. She had suffered with polio as a child and had a true fighting spirit. She was good for me. The kids began making friends, and Jeff enjoyed his job – all 60 to 65 hours a week's worth. It was the best job Jeff had landed in his career, so far, because of all the experience he was receiving. His boss was a pleasure to work with and nonthreatening - a great mentor and a Christian. It provided the healing and confidence that he needed to carry on.

My mom moved to California to be near my brother who had relocated there because of his changing employment.

The following summer, Jeff and I wanted to take the kids and go out to visit my family, but we knew the airfare would be too expensive for all of us to go. One day, I noticed an ad "Buy one ticket and a child can go for $1.00." Did I read that right? This was too good to be true! I immediately called my sister and said, "How would you like to go to California with us if you buy your ticket?" She jumped at the chance, so three adults flew to see my mom with three excited children sitting beside us. We had a great time visiting family.

God allowed us to visit my mom and see how well she had settled-in near my brother after all the trauma back in Indiana. The whole trip helped put me back together and forget the past. Thank you, God. I knew He cared about what had happened when we had to leave my mom behind – my faithful Father, Guide and Songwriter continued His faithfulness to me despite what went on in the world.

Crickets were singing in Greenville, too. They were everywhere but not in my awareness.

After Danny entered kindergarten, I went back to college to recertify my Ohio teacher's license in hopes of returning to teaching. I began subbing in the local schools.

Our daughter, Keri, was in the 5th grade. She needed braces, and Jeff's employment did not provide the coverage. The lousy economy and all the instability had certainly taken its toll, and I wondered how we were going to pay for them. I didn't think – didn't know - to pray about this need, but God sent His provision anyway.

One day, I got a call from one of the neighbors. "I have a friend who is looking for childcare for her little 7-year old daughter before and after school. It is a nice family with a sweet little girl who needs somewhere to go while her mom goes back to work. There are some family issues. Would you be interested?"

After thinking about it, I knew I should help out and said, "Sure."

The amount that she paid each month was exactly the amount that paid for the braces. She came for two years and made a great playmate for my 3rd grade daughter, Kelly. Keri wore her braces for two years.

Thank you, God. He added another note.

Our life in Greenville was very desirable with small-town dynamics, slow-paced and normal. The kids were into sports, friends, parties, and Jeff and I were working. We joined a newly-formed church, interdenominational, and I sang in the choir. Our pastor was a humble man, but great in his knowledge and faith in God and very comforting to me as things began to get more threatening - again.

The company made chrome grills for cars and was struggling to survive much like many other companies in the 80's. It was losing money so it was bought out by another large company. In the back of our minds was the ugly thought of layoffs and plant closings again, all the issues facing workers at that time – events that were only too familiar to us - unpleasant, unsettling, unstable events that tended to rob myself and our family of the American dream that was almost dead to me. Now, it seemed like we were just trying to survive - land on our feet – and were floating along – drifting - while Jeff had to keep paying the high emotional price of fear and pressure to provide for his family.

In four more years, major layoffs began. We survived them all but began to look around for another company that was more stable.

"Here we go again," I thought. This whole corporate thing was becoming very:

uncomfortable
distasteful
scary
threatening
hard
miserable

We were at its mercy as it ran over our lives time and time again.

I began weekly visits to my pastor's office in fear and trembling about the future - trying to find that peace, that inner strength to face it. I was desperately looking for "the answer" to save us - that company - not realizing again that *God* was the answer.

I couldn't hear the crickets faithfully singing their song at night – not yet anyway.

With the knowledge of the company losing money and the future looking bleak, the pressure and worry returned - especially for my husband. Trying to handle working long hours, recovering from a breach from the past and exploring new possibilities was taking its toll on him physically and emotionally. His mother had recovered from colon cancer a few years back, but now liver cancer appeared which multiplied the pressure he carried. She also made it through that surgery successfully and lived to be ninety, but my concern for my husband was there in a big way.

I started to keep a journal. I struggled with great fear and depression as I watched Jeff go through these trials. I wanted out of this whole job mess more than anything in the world! Surely there had to be a company to work for that would solve our dilemma. A company that:

was stable

was trustworthy

was decent

provided a future

Jeff's faithful boss encouraged him to look for employment because of the financial condition of the company, so Jeff began interviewing again. There was no American dream anymore, no real confidence, just a methodical glimmer of hope that, maybe, this time would provide the answer. I had shifted into survival mode.

God seemed to be a million miles away for me. I just didn't know why He wasn't solving our problem. He wasn't giving us "the answer." Something was wrong. So far, we had to move and sell our home every four years and watch companies close down. Three of the four companies that we worked for didn't even exist anymore – gone, evaporated! What was going on in my America? I was tired, disillusioned and wanted the answer:

I really wanted the answer!

I really wanted the answer!

the answer

the answer

I wanted an escape. I wanted this to end. I would solve the problem. I needed to get my teaching job back. It became my driving passion. That teaching job could save us. I could save us.

I still didn't know that the answer and my peace were in God, not in a job.

I was still external and stressed, not getting it and looking to companies to keep us safe – not hearing God's crickets sing:

It's OK.

I'm here.

Don't worry.
I have everything under control.
I am the answer.
You are safe in My arms.
You are secure.
I'll never let you fall.

No, there was no music for me - just numbness and great fear mixed with meager anticipation and great anxiety about what was around the next corner; would it be good or bad for us? I had no real inner assurance and certainly no inner peace.

I met with my humble pastor in the tiny newly founded church down the street at least once a week for his encouragement. He seemed never to be shaken. Why? What was I missing? I wanted that peace.

After our fourth Christmas with the company, the announcement came in January that the plant would close in April. Oh, dear, that was only four months away! No monster for me this time because we knew about the expected financial condition of the company. No dreaded jaws threatening to destroy us. It wasn't so dark because we hadn't been betrayed – stepped on. This was happening to everyone. I just had another chance to look to God - again. Deep inside, I did have a fraction of hope that God would still save us; that He would find our sanctuary and the haven that would keep us safe from the madness of the world until we retired with that gold watch.

I called my pastor with concern about the news. He said with full assurance, "When do you need the job?"

"We need it April 6th," I replied.

"Then pray for April 6th."

That simple? OK. This directive gave me focus and faith. Someday, I wanted to be as confident about God as he was. How did he get that:
faith
strength

hope
confidence
peace
What was the secret?

I wanted that peace and stability more than anything in the world; that desire would be fulfilled, but not until many other events transpired in my life to bring death to myself and my independent spirit. God was building my faith and destroying my flesh - independence. I had to learn how to walk in the Spirit – His Spirit.

God had given us a stay in Greenville for four years. It had truly been a green pasture for me, a place to heal and build up some confidence in business again – in life again – in hope again.

Jeff had gained a lot of valuable experience in those four years. After the announcement in January, he received a desirable possibility with a large, stable company that made cabinets. They had been in business many years, and the job was very appealing to us. He interviewed and was their first choice candidate so more hope was returning to our lives – my life. But in a few weeks, the company decided to freeze the job because of the poor economy.

Jeff's boss offered him a position with a small plant near Greenville, but it was unstable and also losing money.

I kept praying for April 6th.

Chapter 13

The Answer

The job – *the answer* - came on April 8th. Again:
amazing!
wonderful!
whew!
whoa!
humbling!
dodged a bullet!

God added several more notes to my song that day – some of the loudest ones to my deaf ears.

In spite of all my previous fears, doubts and dark thoughts, God continued to be faithful and show His tender mercies again and again and again. God was definitely helping us. He was with us – at least I knew that - during all those times of crisis.

But for me, now, everything had become all about *the answer,* the answer I was searching for, the external - that job - and the hope that God had provided the answer to finally meet this terrible, unsettling problem of job instability that constantly played havoc with our lives both physically and emotionally.

I really believed that - this time - He had delivered us in a mighty way. Look at the date of arrival, right on time, and what

God Didn't Have to Make the Crickets Sing

an answer it was - at least in my eyes. Jeff had been hired by a large manufacturing company that had been in business for years back in our hometown of Newark, Ohio where we started this mad journey of the American dream. We had traveled full circle and were back to square one, our hometown. This company - surely this was going to be the last answer - was a strong company with many years of stability. And I knew that God wouldn't let us down this time – let *me* down this time.

And now, because we were going home, I could get my teaching job back at my old district from many years before. They knew me, and they liked me – like me really well, and my former principal was still the superintendent. How perfect was that? I knew it was hard to get a teaching job and this would be my link – my connection.

After receiving the news about Jeff's job, I immediately picked up the phone and called my past superintendent in supreme and ecstatic excitement.

"Mr. Mills, we're moving back to Newark, and I want to know the chances of getting my old teaching job back? I've been subbing for two years, and I'm ready to get back into the classroom again."

"Of course, your job opportunities are very good. You have a great reputation with the district," was his encouraging reply.

This really *had* to be it - this had to be it – what I had been hoping for, waiting for and dreaming for all these tumultuous years. We were saved again - at the last minute - with this wonderful and promising situation from God. I imagined that I could now save and stabilize our family with my teaching career - save my family so no corporation could *ever* mess with our lives again. And I was determined to make that happen, with every strength and amount of faith in my body.

I wound up sleeping on the couch for a whole week because I literally couldn't catch any z-z-z-z-'s; I was so *excited!* Jeff had been gainfully employed by a tremendously solid company, and

I would get to teach again. This was *the answer* – had to be *the answer*! This answer would pay for our kids' college – a major concern of mine – and provide that stability and retirement we were dreaming of for our future. In my plan, I still had plenty of time to accumulate 30 years of teaching experience in order to retire with a good pension.

Surely, after all this suffering, God had really done it this time. He must have seen us, heard us, noticed all the tears and worry and sent His answer, and I was very, very, very thankful, so very thankful to Him for rescuing us time and time again and now providing us with *the answer*. I believed He had obviously restored us and the deflated American dream. It was certainly not too late for us. I grabbed the external and ran – ran fast and hard with rock-solid faith and expectation.

Ready, set, go – ready, set, go – ready, set, GO!

I was off. Again, we put our house in Greenville on the market and in early June packed up half our stuff and moved to a nice condo in the city of Newark near a private pool. We kept some furniture and nonessential belongings back in our old house until it sold.

The move was difficult for me in some ways:

- Our oldest daughter was entering high school and leaving her close friends and boyfriends behind. She was upset.
- Part of me didn't want to go back to my hometown – it didn't seem the same.
- I felt like all the other wonderful places where we had lived in the past should still be our home.
- We had left many dear Christian friends in the past.
- Mom and Dad weren't there anymore.
- We hadn't sold our house.

But God was still guiding us, and I was full of hope and confidence in this. My American dream had been restored – 150%. I truly felt very blessed, safe and favored by God.

I knew the verse in I Peter 5:10 that said, "... after you have suffered a little while, (God) will Himself restore you and make you strong, firm and steadfast."

I felt like that is just exactly what He'd done:

no more problems

no more moves

no more layoffs

no more plant shutdowns

no more tears

no more pain

no more darkness

no more fear

no more hopelessness

only secure, hopeful and wonderful blessings ahead for our family

external answers, external answers, external answers

external peace – peace in circumstances

During that summer, we didn't know anyone except a few Christian friends from an old Bible study group. We enjoyed the private pool within walking distance from our condo. By the end of the summer, we were all settled in. The kids were all signed up for school. Keri was going to my old high school and Kelly was headed for my old middle school. Jeff loved his job at Rockwell, and I looked forward to getting my teaching position back, hopefully grades three through five.

But in the late 80's, that dreaded downsizing monster was still prowling around with its treacherous jaws seeking to devour anyone in its path. Buyouts, closings and chaos were still the theme for manufacturing in this country.

You would think I could hear the crickets, now, but I couldn't because I was still looking outward for my melody, my peace.

You would think, by now, that I would know that God was my security - everyday. But I didn't. He only answered my panicked prayers. You would think, by now, that I would know there was a safe path for my soul with Him every day and not in these companies. He was the One holding my frightened, vulnerable hand. But I didn't, and I was positioning myself for another huge letdown.

We enjoyed our life very much that first year of Jeff's employment. One beautiful summer afternoon in our condo as I was getting ready to go to the pool with my kids, I received a phone call. It was one of the principals from my old district who I knew. He wanted to know if I'd like to interview for a job; the superintendent had informed him that I'd moved back and told him to call me.

"Hey, Gail, this is Mr. Williams calling. I had a hard time finding your phone number because it isn't listed yet. Anyway, I have a 3rd grade position open. I've already interviewed someone else, but I would like you to come in if you are interested."

Wow! Here it was! This was just

too much

too much

too much

and I was in Heaven, but we had just moved into our small condo. I was still dealing with unpacking and sorting all our things as well as a very upset freshman daughter who felt like her life was over because of the move.

"Bob, if you have already interviewed someone else, why don't you go ahead and give it to her and call me with the next available position," I replied - full of confidence. "My chances of being hired are good, right?"

"Oh, yes, you have a very good reputation with the district."

I had peace. I knew that God had moved us here so I could get my old job back. I wasn't worried at all.

I began subbing in my old district as well as the local city school system where we lived, the system where I graduated - waiting for my job. My former principal, who was now the current superintendent, came to see me during my first substitute teaching assignment in a 1st grade in my old district. That visit was affirming, wonderful and encouraging. It was delightful and somehow comforting to see him again – a familiar face from the past - a reminder of friendlier times, more hopeful and secure times. He had the usual smile on his face when we reunited in that classroom. It felt wonderful, just wonderful – this was exactly what I had desperately hoped for.

Jeff continued working at his Fortune 500 company but didn't have a lot to do. The man he replaced had retired from the company with health issues, and Jeff had been hired in his position. The company had almost decided not to fill the position, but we felt that his new boss wanted to hire Jeff when he discovered that we were from Newark and were trying to get back. For a while everything was:

great
wonderful
working
prospering
unthreatening
stable

Then, one more shock - another disappointing day arrived in February - an old, unwelcomed pattern, a dead dream and a bite – the monster. Jeff had been laid off. After nine months, the horrible monster attacked us again:

company layoffs
company not doing well
company being sold
company doesn't need us any more
making us vulnerable
making us numb

What was left to say? I had *nothing* to say – *nothing but rage*. I was *so angry* at God, at companies, at corporate America, at the American dream and at life in general. I had never felt like this before. There was no more faith - no nothing – just shock and numbness. I was empty – emptied.

I stamped my feet and lashed out, "You are asking us to make bricks without straw!" This whole American dream was *over for me. Really over and I wanted out.* I swore that I would get that teaching job to get us out, to save us, to save my family - to save me. I was so done, so very done with it all! And yet, God wasn't. He was still there patiently:

guiding
protecting
providing
encouraging
taking care of us
in control
holding on

Each night through the difficult winter, the crickets sleep to prepare for their beautiful songs that come in the summer, the songs that come when it is hot, humid and uncomfortable outside. As God kept me safe in His precious, strong arms, I was getting much closer to hearing the crickets sing for me back in my own hometown. But the process hurt and hurt a lot. I just needed to let go and be able to listen.

God was allowing me to be broken - broken of myself, of my flesh, of my independence, of my plans. The external was failing me - failing me badly - all those promises of doing it the right way, college, ambition and all. There was no peace in that. This worldly path was so different and difficult:

broken
crooked
threatening
frustrating
painful

Corporate manufacturing in America was in trouble. The jobs were going overseas. Companies were buying each other out and laying-off workers to show bigger profits. Unfortunately, we were caught right in the middle. We were trapped - just like rats in a cage - the monster circling us without taking its eyes off our terrified faces.

I was furious that God didn't seem to have *the answer* for us. I failed to realize all along that *He was the answer.* He was bigger than corporate America. But I felt like I had lost Him. Where were we supposed to go again? What was I supposed to believe again? This was pointless. There was no desire to pursue any of that dream any more on my part. Uproot my kids – my family - again? No!! Never!! Jeff felt the same way. No more dreams of moving around to find the answer, the company that would fulfill all our dreams for a decent future. Jeff and I were just dead with it – totally dead and wiped out with it all.

But that was OK because my God wasn't dead at all - but alive and well.

Jeff began looking again locally for another job. As we were walking around the block together one day, he made the announcement, "I'm not moving anymore."

I thought and rebelled, "That's just great. Now, we're stuck here and have let the system beat us." My parents had taught me that you have to go where the job is. I would still fight, but with a broken heart.

"But what if we can't find a job here?" I worried.

Unemployment checks began coming in again. We knew how that system worked. We hadn't sold our house in Greenville yet.

I was called to interview in two more of the schools in my old district. I didn't get any of those jobs. One of the rejections was especially crushing to me since I had been asked specifically by that 6th grade teacher to sub in her class quite a few times. That teacher left me a note each time, "Good job today. Everyone likes you."

That June, she resigned, and her job was available - I was available. I interviewed for it, went home and waited for the phone to ring. I waited and I waited and I waited. I stared at the phone as each day passed – laid on the couch staring at the phone for a week; I tried to make it ring – imagined it ringing - dreamed about it ringing. After a week, it still didn't ring, and I gave up.

Then, another opportunity at another school in my old district opened up after a 6 week subbing job. As I interviewed, I was sure I had the job, but, again, it was not to be.

This notion that I would work for my old school district was dead, deader than a doornail and over. It was very disturbing – extremely so. I was rejected and terribly hurt – probably at God as much as anyone else. Where are you, God? What are you doing? I always counted on being able to get back near my old school district where I had taught 5th grade for six years. I just knew that they would hire me back, and I would stabilize and save my family. Apparently this wasn't going to happen.

I was still so lost - away from God's peace that was available to me - His plan, His hope and still looking to the external. There was no job. I only heard the song of my pain, my fear, my intense anger, my desperation and my desire to be out of all this mess around us – but how?

After a year, our realtor called to tell us that the condo, our current place of residence, had been sold, so we had to find another place to live since we still hadn't sold our house. By now, I really felt alone – abandoned and uncared for – certainly on my own and wandering. I felt homeless and rejected - by God and man. Homeless. Jobless. Hopeless.

Where was God?
Where was I?
Where were we going?
What was going to happen to us?

Jeff and I started looking for another place to live. We actually found a lovely condo available near the area where I grew up that was larger and less expensive. It had a finished basement and was out in the country with several others. It was called Countryside and was very nice. We moved into our new location.

My three kids started school in all their excitement. I quit subbing at my old district out of disgust. After the first two days of school, I got a call from the sub service of my local city school system where I graduated many years before.

"Can you sub in a 4th grade classroom today?"

"Sure, I'll be right there."

Ready, set, go –

I was there, and I was engaged and loving being in the classroom. I was always comfortable there. The day ended, and I got the same call the next day, "Can you come in and sub again in that classroom?" Off I went again to sub. That first week I subbed in that room for three days.

The next week, the call came again, "Can you come in again? The teacher is having back trouble, and they would like to keep the classroom consistent with you."

Pretty soon, that classroom teacher faced back surgery, recovery and pain. One month extended into two months. She was unable to return to her classroom because of the serious issues and recovery with her back. After so many consecutive days, the district began paying me base pay with benefits and perks. This assignment lasted six months until February. This situation became our income as the unemployment was running out.

I was so blessed being in that room and enjoying the kids immensely and they me. I basically became their teacher for the majority of the year. I was so hopeful. Now, I *knew* how God was going to get me that teaching job – through this impressive six month subbing position.

Because of the economy, interviewing for a new job was slow, at best, for Jeff, and I just kept my eyes on Jesus and not my depressed, defeated, tired husband who sat on our condo couch day after day looking - waiting for work and feeling like a failure.

When December came, Jeff got a call to interview with Borden, but we heard no real reaction from them about his status. There was no "We'll be in touch," or "We really enjoyed talking to you. You'll probably be hearing from us soon." Jeff wasn't really excited or hopeful about it. It was a small plant outside of Columbus, and it didn't look real stable.

The new year arrived, and I just kept busy teaching and dreaming of getting my teaching job to save our family. I fully expected to be there until the end of the year. That would give us more time to find a job for Jeff. I had it all planned out.

The second week of February arrived. On Monday, the principal called me over the loudspeaker and asked me to report to his office after school had dismissed for the day.

I walked into his office. He asked me to sit down and said, "I just wanted you to know that the classroom teacher is coming back next Monday, so this Friday will be your last day. We really appreciate all you have done for the school and the kids."

It was only the middle of February! I was counting on her being out for the rest of the year so we would have income and benefits. Then, I would get a job with the district and save us. That was *my* plan. **My small chorus of crickets was still sleeping and silent in February.**

I panicked with sick feelings – that hole in my stomach again. No, no, no, this can't happen, God! We won't have anything to live on! Help us! How will we pay our bills? The unemployment had run out, and we would be cut off. I went into fear again. I didn't have enough faith for something so big, so threatening. This was a Goliath, and I sure wasn't a David. I was tired and everything was falling apart. I was a wreck inside. I called my older sister at midnight after everyone was asleep that night in absolute panic, with tears - desperate tears – falling from my eyes.

"All I know is that God said He would take care of you," she encouraged calmly.

Where did these Christians get this inner peace, confidence, assurance – just like my dear pastor back in Greenville? I sure didn't have it – not this type of faith.

I still heard no song. I sure hadn't recognized anything of the melody, nor could I hear any song. I was listening to the wrong tune.

I couldn't because I was still trying to handle life by myself, looking for God to bring that one job that would solve this horrific problem that we had been facing for so many years – the external answer. I was up and down - up and down like a yoyo - riding that emotional roller coaster, and it was exhausting. I was being tested and failing. I was being broken - suffering - and hated it; I wanted to escape.

God was teaching me dependence on Him, and I wanted out - so bad. I couldn't hold onto God anymore. There was nothing to believe. We were just in trouble – always in trouble. We hadn't sold our house yet and now we would be jobless. How much worse could it get, God? I didn't understand how to walk with God in the Spirit. I didn't understand what God was trying to do in all this and why it kept happening. He was just AWOL!

Friday morning came, and I went off to work. I was so numb - totally numb – just going through the motions. The kids in the classroom were sorry to see me go and also some of their parents. Two parents wrote letters of recommendation to the school board trying to encourage them to hire me. We had a little party in the classroom with a few presents of appreciation.

And then it happened, again – my miracle from my faithful God. At the end of that day on that Friday, I received the best present of all. Jeff showed up at the school and came into my classroom while we were finishing the "Good-bye" party.

He smiled - he hugged me. "Borden called, and I start on Monday."

Wow!! Many, many notes added to my chorus.

I was so overwhelmed with relief; it was impossible to believe and almost too good to be true. I was just so glad – so very glad, so very glad that God had answered again - always at the last minute –always when the need was there, just like the pastor had said. I was beginning to learn. This was the very same day as my last day at school.

What do you say to this God of love, faithfulness, and grace? The One who:

keeps me
saves me
sustains me
loves me
hears me
watches over me and my family
waits until the last minute

the One who holds me in the palm of His nail-scarred hands, who never lets me drop and is always there saving me.

I really didn't have anything to say. This faithful answer was really beyond anything I tried to handle or could control. I was just really glad the answer came, and it was over.

God knew that I was getting so close to hearing those crickets sing His song that He had created for me – so close. But there were still some more notes and scales to add.

Jeff had received another external answer – another Fortune 500 company. I told myself, "With Borden, it's got to be good." Meekly I thought, "Hopefully this will be it and provide that future for us." But the seeds of independence and escape had been deeply planted in my soul, and I was driven to get that teaching job - I had to. I saw no other way out of all this madness.

I was still determined to get myself out of this mess, this corporate America mess that had created the American *nightmare* for my family and me. I had been raised to have a strong, self-reliant, independent spirit. I still had some more to learn and experience; that self-reliance needed to break - to die - before the true melody of my Father's song would become part of my inner strength – my real, inner peace for the rest of my days.

Life returned to normal again, as normal as could be for our family. Jeff started working at Borden and brought home free ice cream almost weekly. It was a good working environment, small, laid-back and friendly. We enjoyed this blessing for him - for us. The kids were busy at their schools. Shortly after my six month substitute position ended in 3rd grade at my prior school, I was hired into a six weeks middle school science position to sub for a teacher who had to leave unexpectedly.

When June came, I went to visit a couple of principals that I had subbed for. "I really want a job. I'm a good teacher with references, and I really care about the kids."

They were vague and noncommittal. I got an interview for a middle school English teacher position at the middle school where I had subbed for six weeks, but nothing - no offer - just rejection. I was left high-and-dry again. No leads or interest came my way that summer for a teaching position.

I was still angry. I had been planning – conniving, and it was not working.

I decided to sub at the middle school with a more challenged student body during the next school year. I figured if I made a good name for myself there, I would surely be hired. Not everyone wanted to teach or sub in that building. At that school, I spent an entire school year adding some nice credits to my portfolio and caring a lot about those kids. Teachers at that school were requesting me.

When I was walking into the building one morning, some students said, "We're glad you are here because the kids respect you."

June came, and I told the principal at that middle school that I wanted to be hired in any position. She was encouraging – the usual talking points.

August came with no phone call asking me to interview. I visited the principal to find out what happened.

"Oh, we had two positions open, and we hired two Ohio University students to fill them."

That was *it*!! I had *had* enough. I was done, finished and very angry.

The system had failed me, stabbed me in the back time after time. Schools were notorious for hiring fresh talent, inexperienced teachers from colleges because they were cheaper.

I gave up, really gave up this time. I had so much

resentment

rejection

bitterness

and frustration inside of me. I was a good teacher. I had been requested by teachers, principals and students for subbing jobs, but no one wanted me for a teaching position, and God wasn't opening that door. Why? Here I was, back near my old school district, and they wouldn't hire me back. And the school system that I graduated from was following the same path:

rejected!

not interested!

politically correct answers!

"No!"

"Go away!"

"You'll never get a teaching job," rang the chorus of discouragers from my friends and family. "Give it up!"

But it was a strong desire in my heart, one that would not go away. I loved my profession and the kids even when I was subbing. I desperately wanted back in. I was good at it - had been continually affirmed by my supervisors, parents and students. And God had been with us. Why this negative answer for me?

This teaching position would have solved all our problems of instability and concern over finances.

The scriptures say, "... in all things God works for the good of those who love him...." Romans 8:28

Where was my good? Where were you, God? Why all the lies and rejection?

I would soon find out why.

Chapter 14

God is in Control

Be still, and know that I am God . . . . Psalm 46:10

The crickets had survived the cold winter, and now summer was here with those hot, steamy nights. The crickets were ready to start playing their music again - joyfully and loudly - singing their faithful songs year after year.

Our house in Greenville, Ohio finally sold within two years. We wanted to buy a new one before school started in August. It was important to me that Dan, our son in 3rd grade, remain in the same elementary school, so we wanted to get settled before the end of August.

We began looking for houses around that elementary school. I knew the town since I had grown up in Newark. There weren't a lot of newer housing developments at that time in that area. If I could have picked, I would have picked the older development on top of the hill behind where I grew up. It was really the only place that appealed to me, but I figured that we just couldn't afford the homes.

We found a split-level under construction in another new housing development, but it was small and so expensive for the square footage of the house. I was not very excited about it because it really was quite tiny. We decided that we'd better make a bid on it and get settled rather than lose it.

That weekend, we were all in the basement of our condo watching the housing channel. A house flashed by on the screen that was in that area on top of the hill where I wanted to live in the first place. It was a nice-sized home, a large split-level with a finished basement. And it was listed at the *same price* as the little split-level we were considering - just in time. The house was priced low because the owners were anxious to relocate to the husband's new job – again, a wonderful, faithful, personal accommodation from my precious heavenly Father.

We immediately jumped up, raced to the phone to call our realtor. Within a month, we were happily moving into our 30-year old home on top of the hill behind the house *where I grew up* – just too weird.

Jeff worked for Borden for two years before someone bought the company, divided it up and closed down Jeff's plant. Financial problems, downsizing, plant shut-downs - again - the American theme song of the 80's. But God, in His great mercy, took us straight from employment at Borden on Friday to employment at United Technologies in Zanesville on Monday.

Our ship just kept right on sailing on the violent – tumultuous - sea so full of turbulent storms and threatening waves. Praise God! I just held on tight to our tiny vessel that my God was steering in my life. That Zanesville job lasted two years until a predictable downsizing hit, and Jeff was bumped out of his job by someone else who had more seniority. The plant soon closed down.

This story had become a way of life for us, and God just held on to us - really tight - and kept us on the path – His path –while we watched so many manufacturing jobs being lost at sea as our economy became more global. Somehow, I was learning how to hold on to that stable, invisible Hand - the Hand that I couldn't see - but promised to never let go of me, to never leave me or abandon me. This lesson was hard for me to learn because I was so self-reliant, self-confident, self-assured - a person who had done it all the right way, at least it seemed like that, and had never expected life to be like this.

More notes and measures were being added.

Jeff and I desperately wanted out of corporate America and a few months later, Jeff accepted a job with a small CPA firm in town. He worked there for eight years, and we enjoyed some reasonable stability. Our salary and benefits were limited, but God was faithful to us.

In disgust and frustration with everything I had experienced with teaching possibilities, I went home and started babysitting. While we lived in our condo, I had met an enthusiastic lady who had operated her own child care business for years. I was looking for something and became very interested. She gave me all the ins-and-outs of being successful. It seemed like the only answer for me. I had been frightfully concerned about paying college tuition for three upcoming kids and wondered how we were going to pay for that. My teaching job was supposed to do that. I was desperate to figure out a way to pay for college and save my life.

I was determined to keep ahead of the tsunami that wanted to drown me at every turn. Yes, God had been faithful, but what a ride - what a crazy, threatening ride it had been! God in His faithfulness had kept us so safe and secure as we dragged, trudged, complained and cried along this path looking for our answer - the external job to save us, to provide our future and our hope. After almost 20 years of employment, we were hanging on and just surviving - disillusioned - and not dreaming anymore. The emotional toll on my husband was *huge* as well as my concern about finances for:

college
retirement

bills

My American dream was dead, so dead. Our dreams of the good life and success from hard work had vanished – died a slow, agonizing death.

But the point I failed to realize was that God still had many crickets singing my song all around me, every day and all day.

My God was supplying *His* American dream for us - His blessings of:

a loving family
many good jobs
a great husband
needed finances
some lovely homes
divine protection

He had totally provided for and blessed us – kept us safe and sound - but in *His* way of developing my internal faith, peace and contentment in Him, not an external job. I still failed to recognize it. I hadn't learned to walk in the Spirit, yet; I still didn't know how. God was still working, breaking, teaching, and I was just clueless to the answer that I was really looking for. It was in Him, but I still had more wandering to go through.

Would I ever hear them?

Babysitting was OK. To the average onlooker, it probably looked like a pretty nice setup, a desirable, private business, but to me, it felt like I had been dumped - rejected by the educational profession that I dearly loved, working with the kids that I wanted to help and make learning fun in a classroom.

I had school bus fever in my blood, and I wanted to be there on the first day of school every fall when the school year began. I longed for:

my own classroom
my own desk
my name on the door

the love of my students
the respect from the parents
the summers off
the creativity of lessons
the enjoyment of adult conversation
the stimulation of discussing the latest trends in education
recess
the whole school thing

I developed my babysitting into a professional preschool, "Miss Gail's Preschool Reading Center," with an emphasis on early reading. Our new house with its easy access from the garage to the finished basement was perfectly built for this job. And, I actually *was* teaching every day making learning fun - just not in the way I wanted. Many of the things I needed were provided by grateful parents in my preschool such as car seats, bikes, toys and supplies.

These little tykes were very impressionable, and I knew the importance of being there with them to teach them social skills and early learning concepts, to love them and to teach them about Jesus - how much He loved them. In my preschool, some kids were dealing with divorce. I counseled two distraught fathers who begged me to plead with their wives to seek reconciliation. I worked with children of single moms with unstable family lives. I provided stability and peace for the children of some parents who lost their jobs.

I knew that this was God's work, surely a ministry. But deep inside, I just wasn't satisfied. I just didn't understand the way things were working out at all, or maybe I just didn't like it. I just felt so trapped, imprisoned and cheated when my own kids came home from school, and I was still babysitting until 5:00.

God faithfully provided the maximum number of children allowed in my home and provided a good income for six years in my preschool.

Could I hear the song, yet?

We were new to the city and didn't know many people so this string of steady clients was amazing to me. During the summer, I filled up my six child care spots within six weeks. It just seemed like people always knew someone who needed "a sitter." My preschoolers' parents were so grateful to me for the loving care, discipline and education that I gave to their children, and the kids thrived with me each day.

But, I sat in my finished basement day after day surrounded by my pretty home, gorgeous yard and nice neighborhood wondering why I was in my basement day after day until 5:00 while my own children were home from school upstairs watching TV, and I was stuck with babysitting. I still wanted to be in my own classroom – that freedom with my summers off - that profession. I would babysit to pay for my kids' college, but not for anything else. I was a good teacher; I knew it, and many others knew it too.

Why hadn't God answered this desire? I struggled with bitterness and resentment – stuck in my basement each day away from the adult world. My pride was probably speaking and complaining, "This is not what I want, not what I was promised." I didn't believe that this was God's plan for me at all. I really didn't even know anything about a *plan*. I felt like I had just been dumped. Where was He? I carried deep resentment and bitterness for everyone - including God.

My bitterness of moving back to my hometown, going through more job losses and not being hired by my old school district made my feelings die. I had become very numb. Life had just not worked out. Some tension began developing between Jeff and me. After all, he hadn't helped matters with all those corporate moves and promises that had transpired – not that it was his fault. He didn't really understand what was happening to me. Everyone just seemed to expect something from me and in my resentment - I was rebelling.

I sought some pastoral counseling. I was looking - seeking - to find the answer to prosperity and peace in my inner life and to try and heal spiritually and emotionally.

The chords of the song kept digging deep in my soul, but don't sing any music for me. I didn't want to hear it.

My plan, *my* dream, *my* path had not worked out, and here I was – abandoned, forgotten and rejected by people, career and God - who mattered the most to me.

Jeff was also struggling with broken dreams and promises from life, from corporations and seemingly from God - all the external stuff that doesn't deliver, all the lies that the world tells us about life that we believe and all the deceptions that our enemy whispers in our ears. Things were becoming tense for us and our marriage.

I remembered a thought way back in Indiana:

"I'm going to use Jeff's job in his spiritual life."

That seemed to make sense as I watched both of us deal with inner hurts, doubts and frustrations that had been building for years. Instead of rejoicing in the faithfulness of our God, we were bitter and resentful of these plans that did not seem to work out. My pride was hurt. It had been awfully hard.

As I sought counseling, a friend said to me, "But God is in control."

What! I had never heard that before.

"You mean God wanted me to babysit?" I asked in irritating unbelief. This notion of sovereignty would take some thought.

I had always known that God spun the planets into motion, watched over me – I guess – and knew I was alive. I had seen Him race to help me when I got myself into a jam. I never had a clue that He was actually – personally - intricately involved in the little things, controlling the course of my daily life and changing me into the image of His Son – my inner man, my soul. This didn't mean that I lost my free will, but He used it all to help me learn to depend on Him. My life was the perfect, lovely stitching on my embroidered picture with the tangled ends all underneath. Of course, I could only see the tangled ends.

. . . in all things God works for the good of those who love him . . . Romans 8:28

There was that promise, and it gave me great comfort - great comfort.

I was learning that:
He was in control.
He was enough.
He was always with me.
He was watching over me each day.
I would never fall off a cliff.
There were beginnings and ends to trials.
I could relax.
I could stand on His word.
I could let Him worry about my next move.
I was moving through any darkness to the light.

He was in control; this truth hit me in a wonderful, life-changing way. He was driving the car, and I needed to stay in the back seat to see where *He* was going to take me and not where *I* wanted to take me.

I pondered this truth and let it sink deep into my soul. There was Someone there who I could look to each day and have genuine peace if I kept my focus on Him. I didn't have to be afraid of any monsters looming in the dark to destroy me - anymore.

I also watched my husband struggle with brokenness and move towards healing. With some counseling from our pastor, he took his trials and gave his thoughts, worries and hurts to God in a big way. I can honestly say it was the first time I saw something - real - in Jeff's spiritual life. He had become dependent and obedient to the Lord. I saw a genuine compassion for others, a desire to get into Bible study and a change in his inner man. Instead of fear, I heard about his faith and obedience that produced blessing. Our relationship improved in a drastic way, and I felt that the thought that came to me back in my kitchen in Indiana had come true - "I'm going to use Jeff's job in his spiritual life." It had also worked in mine.

Chapter 15

Miracle

> . . . in quietness and trust is your strength . . . .
> Isaiah 30:15

I was pretty much resigned to the fact that I could pay for college by babysitting, and that I would never get my heart's desire – to be back in the classroom with students. Jeff's job seemed like an oasis at the small CPA firm, and things were just OK - I guess; at least we were in a circumstance that was working and meeting our financial obligations - seemingly, pretty secure.

But deep inside, I still hadn't accepted my station in life - a babysitter. I really had a poor attitude, I guess. Many folks would have given a lot to be in our shoes at that time because we were making it and our needs were met; but there were still my shattered dreams and wounded emotions. I went through my daily routine still remembering the times when I had my summers and holidays off and wishing I were back in that classroom somewhere, somehow. I really don't know why this was such a big deal for me, but it was. It was an unmet desire – deep inside of me. It was what I was trained to do – educated to do – what I enjoyed and what I still wanted.

One summer day, Jeff and I went to a baseball game to see our son, Danny, play. We were sitting in the bleachers behind a teacher who I knew who taught in a school district in the county, a teacher who had taught for years. As she was talking, I overheard her say:

"Yeah, we have a new principal, and he is going to hire six teachers."

My ears perked up – six teachers!

I tapped her on the shoulder and asked abruptly, "Did you say six teachers?" I found out where the building was; it was in the county, and off I went the next day as fast as I could.
Ready, set, go –

I discovered that I was still determined to try. I got to the building and walked into a very friendly and inviting, informal principal's office - messy desk and all - to begin a six year journey with him. It was the middle of June, and he was working at his desk.

With my resume and portfolio in hand, I greeted him, "Hi, my name is Gail Carpenter, and I know Mrs. Morris. She said that you might be hiring six teachers. I am very interested in those positions and am a very good teacher. I have my references and picture portfolio right here. Mr. Mills is my main reference."

"Really, Dave Mills and I are good friends!" he looked up smiling with some interest. "Tell me something about yourself."

We chatted for a few minutes. I felt accepted and relaxed.

"Leave your stuff on my desk, and I'll get back with you next week. I'll call Dave."

I left his office. Wow! Wow! Double wow!! This might work out. Hope, hope, hope churned like a fire in my heart. This dream wasn't dead after all. Could this possibly be *the answer*?

I returned exactly a week later. He was in his office again.

"Did you get a chance to look at my stuff and check my reference?"

He replied, "No, frankly, I didn't, but I'm going to call Dave Mills - right now."

While I stared in disbelief, he picked up the phone and dialed Dave's phone number. He chatted for a few minutes.

He hung up the phone, picked up a pencil and said, "Dave says you are top-notch, a great teacher. I have five people on this list, and I am going to put you as number six. I'll fill the jobs in order."

Shock! Shock! Shock! Anticipation! Anticipation! Anticipation! Hope! Hope! Hope! This was unbelievable! This could really happen. I was going to get that teaching job – just out of the blue – with a person and district I had never worked for. Wasn't that just like God? The miracle – my heart's desire - was really going to happen, and I had proved that faith in God does work.

I raced home in the car, carefully avoiding any police cars and pedestrians and told everyone that I was going to get my job. Faith worked, and God was being faithful to me. I was going to be able to stabilize and save us - no more worries.

The external answer had come

I didn't hear anything back that summer about a job. I called Mr. Barnes the next summer to see what was going on. He said that he didn't have anything but was keeping me in mind.

"I've still got you on my list," he said. "I just don't have anything."

That was all I needed to hear to keep me motivated and full of faith – and hope.

The second summer after our meeting, he called, "I've got an art position for you if you want it. You seem very creative and would be good for it. It involves both schools, so you will have to interview with the other principal."

Fair enough. I set up a time with the other elementary school and showed up all decked out in my interviewing clothes. The other principal was an attractive lady who welcomed me in her office. I felt very relaxed and confident to show her my portfolio.

As we began talking she asked, "Why are you interviewing for an art position? It seems like you would be better suited for a Title I reading job. Let's talk about that."

That change was certainly fine with me – anything to get me back in the classroom was fine with me - anything, anything. The interview went very well, and I was sure that I had the job when I left.

"I'll just need to check your references and get back with you in a week," she noted as I left.

I stepped out of that old school building with a heart pounding with excitement. But as the familiar pattern played itself out, I didn't get that phone call from her. I went back a week later to find out what had happened.

While I listened in dismay, she flatly explained, "I couldn't get ahold of Dave Mills your reference, so I called someone else that I knew who I thought might know you, and she said that you were not a team player."

I was so burned out with the public school system and their discouraging policies that I just didn't care to find out who it was. I knew it wasn't true, and I didn't feel like arguing with her but assured her that this was not the case at all. I thanked her for her time.

As I drove home, I thought, "OK where did *that* come from – that lie – that untruth? Who was the person?" I didn't have a clue. I had subbed, taught and tutored for 11 years and had never had a complaint. Why was this path always crooked - a mystery - frustrating? Why was it so hard for God to give me this job? Why the tease? What was wrong with me?

I called Mr. Barnes and told him what had happened hoping that he wouldn't buy the lie. He still encouraged me and hung on to my name. So I knew that God had not closed this door. I was still in great faith that God was going to do this – get me that teaching job. This whole relationship with Mr. Barnes was so peculiar, so encouraging, so interesting and so hopeful that I knew God's hand was with me in this.

Two more years went by. I kept checking in each summer to find out when my position would open up from God. I had been very encouraged and was hopeful. I was a teacher:

a trained professional
good with children
caring about their learning
not accepting their failures
good with parents
an experienced teacher

During the fourth summer, Mr. Barnes called, "I have a part-time kindergarten that you may have. Do you have your kindergarten certification?"

Yes, I was certified to teach kindergarten, but I was making twice the money babysitting that the kindergarten position offered, and we needed my money for college. "Oh, Mr. Barnes, I would love to take it, but I can't afford to quit babysitting unless your position is full-time. I have two girls in college."

He thanked me, softly excused himself from the conversation and hung up. I could tell that my hope had just been snuffed out like a lighted candle in a big way.

Trapped again, trapped by babysitting:
removed from the world
stuck in my basement
frustrated
discontent
bitter

My one, real chance, and I had to turn it down.

By this point, my prayers for teaching were over. I was pretty defeated – very defeated. Babysitting was fine – provided what we needed – and I enjoyed working with the preschoolers. But I still wanted a job that:

was steady
was more professional
was in a school setting
had benefits
had retirement
had time off
teamed with other teachers
offered some freedom

My teaching ship was sunk. I had drowned – down at the bottom of the educational sea. It really was over this time. God had closed the door, and I was resigned to accept it. However, it made no sense to me that this dear principal would just call and offer me jobs for six years, and then God just end it. It made no sense that this principal would even be that interested in me. But if that was God's answer, so be it - I could live with it.

I didn't hear any notes – stanzas – song.

I just saw a bunch of sweet kids playing and learning at my house. That was the best I could do. I quit my job to stay home with my own children years ago, and I never regretted it for one second. I wouldn't trade those days of bonding, fun and being there with them for anything! If I was poor, I would be poor, if I had to babysit, I had to babysit - it was worth it.

That next summer, I ran into an old colleague who used to teach Head Start with me walking down one of the aisles at the grocery store. As we passed each other, we stopped to catch up on our lives. After all the familiar questions and conversation, she asked me, "Are you teaching somewhere?"

I sighed, "No, I can't get a job. I'm operating a preschool in my house with six children. No one is going to hire me."

She replied, "Oh, that's just not true. Our principal is looking for a 1st grade teacher, and you would be perfect with your preschool experience. He really likes more experienced talent - really. Call him and tell him that you know me, used to work with me and what you are doing right now. Ask if you can have an interview for the 1st grade position."

Frankly, she had to talk me into it. I went home, and I called her principal. He was encouraging and set up an interview. It was very positive, and I was actually treated with some genuine interest and respect.

Then he said, "Well, here is where we are. I've already interviewed someone for the 1st grade position and probably need to give it to her. But you are perfect for kindergarten. Our teacher will be retiring next year, and I would like to hire you in that position. Please check back with me around the first of the year."

In guarded amazement, I thanked him feeling very heartened and wondering about this new path that was opening up. Could this dream really be resurrected and happening again?

"Hum, looks like I might have a job. Could it be possible, Lord?" I was guarded, but hopeful again. I knew that I could help kids in public school. God had reenergized my passion, my desire – a desire that I had dreamed of and hoped for.

Here it was again, the promise of a teaching job. It just would not die. The door just wouldn't close, and now I believed, again, that God was still in this – going to give me a teaching job. I felt very encouraged and that maybe I had given up too fast.

Because of this positive experience and promise, I had the tenacity to call Mr. Barnes back one more time and say, "Hi, Mr. Barnes, this is Gail Carpenter calling again. I am still very interested in a teaching job and was just wondering if you have any full-time positions available?"

I could tell by his voice that he had lost interest in me.

"Well, I might have a Title I job next spring. Call me back then."

I hung in there. I was following a path. "Thank you, I will call you back in April," I said meekly and less sure of myself.

The year went by, and I didn't think much more about it. But there was still a small – miniscule – glimmer of hope in my heart that God was still going to get me that teaching job, and I just had to persevere in my quest to get it. I still really wanted a job to provide a financial future and the stability of income for us instead of the ins-and-outs of childcare and the insurance premiums that we had to pay for ourselves.

April came, and I called Mr. Barnes. "Hi, Mr. Barnes, I'm calling because I am very interested in that Title I job that you said might be available this year."

In a dull, very noncommittal voice, he replied, "Yes, call me the day after school lets out in June, and we'll set up an interview."

I knew it didn't feel right, but I had hope that finally this tease was going to end. After all, he *had* offered me positions in the past.

The day after school let out, I got dressed for the interview. I wondered, "Was this really going to happen?" I was pretty numb about the whole thing by now and nervous. I didn't have the self-assurance that I had when we returned to Newark nine years before.

I started the car, pointed it north, and off I went to learn of my fate. I sang hymns with all my might – loud - to keep my nerves quiet and my mind focused on the Lord while I drove there to fight the spiritual warfare going on in my emotions about this desire of my heart. What would it be like to actually get a job? Would I still know what to do? It had been so long. It had been such a battle to get back into my career.

I pulled up in the front driveway of the school. I really was very mindless by this point – sort of just going through the motions. I walked in that familiar office that I had visited a few other times. There was Mr. Barnes sitting on the secretary's desk meeting me face-to-face. "You'll be interviewing with four teachers in there."

He pointed to a side room, the principal's office, and as I turned left to walk in, I thought "You're going to make me interview for this, and you're not going to hire me." It was all too familiar just like the run-arounds from the past." I knew that he was just going to brush me off like everyone else had done.

I sat down to face four friendly smiles. Two of the teachers I knew from previous subbing jobs that I had done in my city school system. Mr. Barnes had hired them. How wonderful for them. We had the usual, comfortable discussion with some questions and comments. They thank me and said the usual, "We'll let you know."

Before I walked out, I turned and made one final plea, "One parent told me that I had done more for her child then two psychologists and three teachers. I would really appreciate this job because I'm having a hard time getting back into the system. I've been told that I'm a good teacher."

We all shook hands and I walked out:
deflated
discouraged
hopeless
knowing that I had just gone through a formality, and I was not going to be hired in that job. I just knew it by the way Mr. Barnes had acted when he greeted me – short and sweet.

I got in my car and started the engine. I drove out of the driveway looking up at the heavens through my tears - exclaiming, "I just don't understand!" Why the six years of hope? Why the encouragement from my friend at the grocery store? Why all the promise? Why would God not let me be hired?

It was over for me, again, just over. I knew my journey of hope with Mr. Barnes had ended, and I didn't understand any of it. All the:
rejection
passion
politics

anger

What was God up to, or was He up to anything? Where was He in all this, and why had it dragged on so long with the door never shutting? It would have been very easy for Mr. Barnes to just brush me off - at first - by saying, "Well, I'll keep your resume, but we really don't have anything available in the near future." But he didn't do that. He had offered me two jobs.

I didn't realize at the time, but God was using every bit of my frustration, rejection, anger and hurt to create a love and a passion for a very special bunch of kids that I was soon to meet.

I went back home and called the other district that had "wanted me for kindergarten" only to hear, "Well, the teacher has decided to stay on for another year."

That was dead too – deader that a doornail.

Just give it up, Gail. *Just give it up!* It's dead, dead, dead, dead . . . !

I decided to just enjoy the rest of the summer with the four preschool kids that I was watching. We went swimming, walking, picnicking – just had some fun. I was concerned because two of the kids were dropping out in August to go to kindergarten which cut down on my income. God had always been faithful to bring in six children to my preschool at the last minute, but this part of babysitting was what bothered me the most. The money was paying for my two daughters' college expenses, and I was very much dependent on God to provide the children - He always did.

There was that word again – dependent. It always felt uncomfortable to me, and I really had a struggle with resting in it.

God had always proved Himself wonderful and faithful in my journey in life, but it still felt uncomfortable – still was external – still no cricket songs.

I didn't experience the peace that He wanted me to have – the contentment, the confidence.

When August came, I decided to contact a small charter school with at-risk kids to see if they had anything. The pay seemed low – less than I currently made – but at least they had benefits. I knew the acting principal.

"Hi, Mr. Johnson, this is Gail Carpenter. I'm calling to see if you have any teaching positions for this coming year?"

He replied, "Why yes, we have a 4th grade, and you would be great for it!"

We set up an interview for that Friday. I was pretty sure that I would get it. The school was small and in a church with disadvantaged children. I wasn't really excited about it, and I wasn't sure about the money. But it just seemed like the right thing to do. It had benefits and was stable.

It was Wednesday around 10:00 in the morning - ten days before school started. I was sitting on my basement steps watching the kids playing and thinking about my interview for 4th grade on that coming Friday.

Suddenly the phone rang. It was Mr. Barnes. "Gail, this is Mr. Barnes. "Do you have a teaching job yet?"

I answered, "No, but I have an interview set up with a charter school on Friday for a 4th grade."

He continued, "Well, this is your last chance. I have a newly-created DH class that you can have if you want it. Other people want it, but you may have it. I need to know right away."

"DH, DH, DH! What's that?" I thought in great anxiety and apprehension. I didn't know anything about DH or what this class would be like. I teetered between trembling and stammering – my knees shaking profusely. This had come completely out of the blue after all hope seemed to be gone, and I was stunned.

Decision, decision, decision!

Right now, right now, right now!

Big change, big change, big change!

Last chance, last chance, last chance!

My heart was pounding, and my head was spinning.

"Yes, I'll take it!!!" I choked.

"Meet me at the school at 2:00, and I'll show you your room and get you signed in."

I hung up in complete shock and disbelief –complete shock and disbelief - complete shock and disbelief. I had just experienced a true resurrection of a dream.

I drove out to the school at 2:00. I saw a motorcycle coming down the highway towards me. It was Mr. Barnes and my introduction back into the educational system. He was welcoming, friendly and excited. I was literally sleep-walking. I signed in and completed all the formalities;

saw the classroom

got the keys to the building

toured the building

met the janitor

learned some procedures

I drove home in such a state of numbness, astonishment and incredulity for I knew that I had just experienced a miracle. God had just knocked my socks off!!

I walked in the door of my house. My husband was lying on the couch watching TV. I dangled the school keys in front of me to show my disbelieving husband. The Red Sea had just parted for me, and I had witnessed the hand of God. God had met my faith, and I was *overwhelmed* with His presence – *totally overwhelmed, totally overwhelmed, totally overwhelmed.* . . .

Many, many notes were practiced in my chorus that day.

Chapter 16

A Turn of Events

After I was hired, Mr. Barnes said, "Frankly, I had forgotten all about you. There were others who wanted this job, but your name just popped into my head."

That comment affirmed to me that God was in this, and it overwhelmed me again. He said that he wanted a positive person because the building staff was so negative.

"You've got the right person for that," I chortled back.

"And no complaining about the size of the room," he commanded.

"Never!" I agreed. I would have gone to the moon if he would have asked me to. I was completely on board - and a nervous wreck.

I had no idea of the blessing that God had put in my path on that particular day in my life. I was so thankful - overcome with the immensity of His answer - and very excited about this opportunity. My life was soon to change in a monumental way, and my heart would be forever warmed by nine very special DH students. God was going to use all the:

pain
hurt

frustration
anger
rejection

that I had experienced to help me identify and relate with some very special, needy kids that I would have the privilege of teaching for two years. Because of my frustrations and rejections from the schools in the past five years, I felt much of their pain of being an outsider - "different"- and rejected by many of their peers and teachers. I had experienced the hurt of it all and understood their anger.

All along, God had His plan to get me a teaching job, but certainly not in the way I would have expected. He was preparing:
the kids
the class
my heart
my instruction
my passion

and all I could do was follow the path – His path.

The kids ranged from 2nd to 5th grade. None of them really knew *anything* academically:
no reading
no math
no spelling
no writing
no nothing
just blank slates looking at me, waiting for me to teach them something - anything.

My life would never be the same.

And all that timing in God's plan was specifically designed to get me ready to be with those kids - for great good. Three of the children were severely delayed in their learning with short-term memory issues and poor abstract thinking skills while everyone else could learn. One of the kids had Turrets Syndrome and slept a lot with his head down on the table. I realized that he had been medicated to help everyone around him cope. I needed him to be awake, so we had his medication changed.

The room was teeny-tiny and divided in half. I shared my half with another intervention specialist. I literally sat backed into a corner near the window at a table all day, squeezed in with nine sets of eyes from eager children staring back at me in their little chairs on the other side of the kidney-shaped table. There was no walking room.

Most of them had experienced difficulty and frustration the previous year at the school as regular classroom teachers tried to figure out what to do with them. They had been in regular classrooms which were not working out to meet the educational and emotional needs of these kids. A couple of kids had just been neglected. And they all sat there looking at me except for the one who was asleep. Probably to the average neophyte entering into this situation, it would have produced fear and a question as to what to do with them all. But to me, God beautifully revealed the whole plan and program for their advancement and acceptance.

My intervention specialist mentor said, "Just do what you did in preschool."

OK, that would be easy enough, and I knew it could work. After all, no one told me these kids couldn't learn. I had no preconceived notions, no training in special education which probably worked to my advantage – and theirs. I expected them to learn, and we began with letter "A."

"A" is for apple.
Monday, color an "A" and practice making capital "A" and lower-case "a" letters.
Tuesday, color an apple tree and practice writing the letters.
Wednesday, make an apple tree out of colored paper.
Thursday, make apple pie.
Friday, play my Apple Game.

Each day, I wrote a paragraph about apples on the board, and the children traced the same paragraph about apples that I had written on their own sheet of paper.

We did some math – touch math – which one of the kids showed me. I loved that math strategy. We also did science. The agenda was set, and the kids began to learn and thrive.

Mr. Barnes advised me that I needed to take classes to stay with that special education class since I did not have that certification. With an uncertain future in that position, I immediately signed up for classes. All of this:

new job
new kids
taking classes
pleasing a principal
learning about IEP's

was a bit overpowering, especially the classes and the pleasing the principal part. I was literally thrown back into the whole educational mix - and I loved it.

Even though Mr. Barnes was very friendly and encouraging, I definitely carried a sense of intimidation and anxiety, at first, being completely out of my comfort zone for so many years, not from working with the kids, but pleasing the teachers and principal. Also, taking college classes was really an unfamiliar, emotional adventure to overcome. What if I couldn't pass? What about tests? Money? I hadn't been back to college in many years, and these classes really counted to keep my job. There was a lot to think about and a lot to worry about.

One day when I was walking down the stairs at the school, a thought popped into my head, "Follow the path and leave the results to Me." This thought was so profound and calming that I wrote it down and taped the paper to my refrigerator. It's still there today, and I am reminded and heed its direction daily to keep my peace and my focus.

It was a wonderful and amazing year of continued praise from their parents and the principal for the progress those kids were making. Many times the principal said:

"Everyone likes you."

"I'm so glad that you kept calling back."

"Hiring you was one of the best things I've done in my career."

"I've had another complement about you today."

"Your old district really missed out by not hiring you back."

I just didn't understand the big deal. I was just a teacher who was enjoying working with my kids. The dream, the answer – my answer - had really come true and in a huge way. God had really come through with the answer I was desperately hoping for; the Red Sea had parted, and I was walking through on dry ground with:

job stability

financial stability

career stability

retirement stability

benefit stability

my emotional stability

To me, I was singing about this job. After all, this was the answer - this job. It was all about this job – a teaching job. And the crickets were outside singing too. But they were singing about something different.

It had all been answered in this wonderful job, and I loved every minute of it. I looked forward to going to work each day. I went to school on Sundays to prepare the reading lessons for the different groups. I bonded to those kids and their parents in a huge way. I loved what I was doing.

Whatever these kids lacked in intellectual capacity, they compensated immensely with their love and affection for me. The three who were more severely and intellectually challenged taught me so much. These guys were people - regular people - like everyone else. Their bodies just didn't function so well. One of them came in everyday with a big smile on his face, full of enthusiasm about the newest animal books that I had gotten from the library that week. He had a great work ethic - always positive and excited - and loved the activities that we were doing each day.

One day as he pranced into the room, I asked him, "Doug, are you ever unhappy?"

"Nope," was his happy and confident reply.

I thought, "If only the entire world could be like him, what a great place it would be."

The rest of the kids were delayed in some way, speech delays, intelligence delays or social delays through neglect. But these guys made great strides in their reading abilities in two years which became my main focus. Two made it to grade level in two years causing one to be reassessed from DH to LD and four made steady progress in reading much to their parents' and the principal's extraordinary delight. Mine also.

I took college classes my first year and stayed with those nine very special kids for two wonderful years. Other students came down to the resource room for various helps, at times, but the original nine were with me all day.

I cannot explain how marvelous this classroom experience was for me and how it drastically changed my life and theirs. These kids had a lot going against them. In time, I fell in love with helping those children, their parents and what I could do to teach them. "You took the most difficult kids and changed their lives," the principal proclaimed a few times.

The second year, I was moved to a portable classroom which was so much better. We were able to move around and be comfortable.

A boy named Joe was placed in my class by his grandmother because of the success and care his sister had received the year before. He was in the 5th grade at another school in a multihandicapped classroom washing tables at lunch. He was a big kid with a bad attitude and way behind in his schooling. He had been neglected and was, apparently, being passed through the system. The schools either didn't know what to do with him or just had set the bar too low. Joe knew nothing about reading when he was transferred and placed in my DH classroom. He knew no letters. He knew no sounds, and he certainly couldn't read - he was in the 5th grade! As a result, he was angry and discouraged, sarcastic and defeated when we met. He thought that he was "stupid" and carried those terrible feelings of worthlessness inside. I guess I was the only one who would believe in him because I hadn't *learned* that he couldn't achieve.

We began learning the letters and sounds of the alphabet and blending. He made slow progress - very slow progress - but he *was* learning and gaining knowledge. The next year, after I left the special education classroom, Joe's grandparents brought him and his two sisters to my house for private tutoring for five more years. Those students continued to gain successful reading skills in word attack and comprehension at my house. Joe's last Individualized Educational Plan noted that he was reading at a 7th grade level! We read the book *Hatchet* which was an upper-elementary reading level book as we were finishing private tutoring.

Meeting Joe made a huge impression on me. I couldn't believe that the system would just allow him to be moved through without serious effort and concern to help him. Maybe the system didn't know what to do or how to teach reading to him, or maybe their opinions of some students were just too negative – lost causes in many teachers' eyes. Whatever it was, I am convinced that Joe would not be reading today if our paths had not crossed.

I was shocked, thrilled and angered all at the same time about what was happening to so many kids and their parents. These students were failing, made to feel stupid and blamed for the problems instead of, perhaps, the way we were teaching them. I thought, "This is NEVER going to happen on my watch again. That kid would not be reading if our paths had not crossed."

My second year ended way too soon, and Mr. Barnes retired. We had worked so closely together and both understood the miracles that had occurred in that small DH classroom. I knew I would miss his support - dearly. As a result of his leaving, I decided to move on to another classroom.

As school was closing, a disturbing form of miscommunication occurred with the district's superintendent. He thought that I was staying with the DH kids, and I thought that I was being transferred to another room to match my K-8 certification. I had decided not to take the classes at the college and several times during the year, I had discussed this option with my principal and the superintendent; there seemed to be an agreeable understanding that I would be moved to a classroom when Mr. Barnes retired. But by May, apparently the superintendent thought that I was continuing to take classes. Somehow this miscommunication created irritation with the administration which I didn't understand and felt bad about – like I had done something wrong.

I took a Title I position and transferred to the other elementary school. As the year ended, Mr. Barnes expressed his appreciation for the fabulous experiences we had both had working together to help my nine DH students. It certainly made his year much easier. For me, I had entered a journey of fulfillment in what my kids were learning - a job where I really made a difference; it truly was the highlight of my teaching career

Even though this was a necessary change, thinking of the move to another school was extremely difficult for me because my heart still belonged to those students, their parents and their progress; it had been amazing! Still, I had no choice but to move on to another situation unless I spent four years taking college classes. It was a very, very difficult transition for me.

One afternoon as the last days of school were playing out, Mr. Barnes called me into his office. "I just wanted to warn you about office politics. Not everyone is friendly to you in this building, and I just want you to be aware."

Whoa, *this* was certainly unsettling and troubling! How could such a successful two years have any problem connected with it? Who would care about me or what I did in that special education room? Why would anyone really care about what I was doing when the two years had obviously been successful? Mr. Barnes, my cooperating classroom teachers, my fellow team teachers and my aides were all very relaxed and enjoyed working as a team with me. I suspected nothing – why should I? Why, I had never experienced anything like this - a sinister event in my life as a teacher – a disgruntled colleague. I was just so naive. I had never suffered under office "politics" before. If anything, I had always enjoyed a trusting, desirable relationship with the other teachers and principals.

I kept that thought under my hat as I moved on to the other elementary school in August. The principal at that elementary school was new. The school was under a lot of pressure to make adequate yearly progress for No Child Left Behind. As I made this change to a new building with unfamiliar faces and walked down the halls into my new world at this elementary school, my heart remained at the other school. There was a sense of numbness about this change. The old familiar acceptance, appreciation and praise from my former boss were gone. I missed the magical wonder of the prior two years under Mr. Barnes, the kids and their parents. But, I was still ready to begin again and make this change happen for me and the students under my care.

The first year in Title I reading and math began without a hitch. After having my room switched three times during the first month of school, I was off to a great start. The principal and

I seemed to hit it off. I didn't have much contact with her other than passing her in the halls or outside on the playground with a friendly, "Hello." I worked with three 4th grade teachers and a 3rd grade class. I supported whatever they did in the classroom by either creating lessons, worksheets, games or doing the assignments that the teachers had already prepared. I did math and reading with the six students from each of the 4th grade classes. I enjoyed my job and the kids immensely and worked to see them gain in their skills – and they did.

My Title I mentor and the teachers were all pleased with my work. I worked tirelessly to help these students become successful in their subjects because I knew the great successes that I had seen two years before as an intervention specialist.

The next year, my contract was up for renewal, and I had no concerns about it what-so-ever. Why should I? I had never – ever - experienced any issues with my work before. At this principal's suggestion, I had signed up and was now working towards my Master's in reading at Muskingum College, keeping a 4-point average in order to satisfy some requirements with the new NCLB law of being Highly Qualified.

Again, I remained in Title I reading teaching kindergarten, 1st and 3rd grade students and working with four teachers. I moved to a nice, spacious portable classroom that I shared with a special education teacher. The whole arrangement was quite desirable, and everyone seemed happy and pleased.

In her evaluation for renewal of my license, there were some good experiences and, yet, experiences began developing of the principal's unsettling concern for me. There just seemed to be some lack of confidence and suspicion about me from the very beginning as I worked more closely with this new principal. Maybe it was her management style, but her overreactions were problematic and created much stress for me. She really made huge mountains out of molehills and really didn't listen well. A lesson I created on main idea in 3rd grade disturbed her in a

God Didn't Have to Make the Crickets Sing

mighty way when it was obvious that the children understood the lesson and the concept being taught. I was instructed to reteach the lesson using different materials. I did.

She began expressing serious concerns to me of my knowledge. I felt her concerns were unfounded and revealed a basic lack of trust in me – something I wasn't used to. Something was just not right. Why was there suspicion about me, about my knowledge and about my judgment? It was almost like some sort of negative impression – shadow - followed behind me to that school, an impression which I didn't understand and was very:

unfamiliar
unsettling
disturbing

Could this be what Mr. Barnes was talking about? I was always aware of the warning that he called to my attention, but I kept this warning to myself - and to God.

I decided to use an alphabetic song with my kindergarten children that I had made up at my preschool and had used successfully in my DH class that was extremely effective in helping kids learn the ABC letters and sounds. I was eventually told by this nervous principal not to sing that song or say the sounds of the letters – only the names of the letters – "a" is for "apple." I did as I was told, but never believed that this was appropriate.

That year, I also worked with six transitional 1st graders. I was blamed for a lesson to my 1st graders that I didn't create nor particularly like. As she observed, the principal said the lesson was "over their heads." I had been told by the teachers to use the same prepared reading lessons that were given to the rest of the 1st grade classes. Their reading books were leveled, the phonic sheets were not relevant to their books; they were not making progress.

Overall, meeting with the union, the principal and I worked out all of her concerns that year. It seemed like I had finally gained her confidence and trust and everything had settled down. I was pleased since my track record from the past two years in the district teaching DH was outstanding and the superintendent knew it. He had praised my work as "outstanding." I knew there was just nothing to worry about.

I was passionate to apply the same methods of phonetic instruction for my 1st graders that I had used in my DH class because I knew that type of instruction would help those children. I sought permission from the principal, and she allowed me to begin writing some story lessons. Almost effortlessly, I wrote one a week in a repetitive, systematic method introducing one word family a week and a few high-frequency words. This simplistic, systematic method proved to be highly effective in helping my six struggling 1st grade readers succeed in their reading abilities.

I showed the principal the new story lesson every week, and she nodded her approval without much comment or interest. I knew the stories and the lessons were wonderful. I loved this time of teaching these story lessons to my children each day. I guess I didn't realize how much I enjoyed helping struggling readers and how successful I seemed to be. The students gained confidence, started volunteering and raising their hands - and smiling. I loved it as I watched them progress. Parents began writing notes showing their excitement about how well their kids were doing.

By the end of the second year at my school, the superintendent wanted to abolish one Title I position. Since I was the newest member of the Title I team, I volunteered to move into a 5th grade classroom teaching primarily math. I had six years of experience in 5th grade and especially loved teaching math.

That move proved to be a mystery - a disaster - but another detour in God's crooked path. God was still in control of my life and full of surprises to His unsuspecting child. He was still working in my life, teaching me to trust Him and digging the notes of His love deeper into my internal soul so I could eventually hear His love song someday. I needed to hear it if I was ever going to find inner peace and experience the fruit of the Spirit in my life.

By this time, the crickets were waiting and practicing in my backyard for me to hear my melody. And it wouldn't be much longer until my ears would be opened.

I needed one more pierce – a huge, empty space - to be created in my heart, and God was well on His way to making that happen - whether I liked it or not.

Chapter 17

The Mystery

> Trust in the Lord with all your heart and lean not on your own understanding; Proverbs 3:5

    Some say that God works in mysterious ways. This was an understatement as far as my year in 5th grade was concerned. A hopeful desire - a fulfillment of my hopes and dreams - began disintegrating right before my eyes, slipping right through my fingers like sand spilling through an hour glass. And as much as I tried to catch the falling granules, I could not stop them.

    My year in 5th grade remains a mystery, one that I still don't understand to this day. It began as a year of confidence and praise from my principal to collapsing into a year of dreadful suspicion and concern within four months about my performance. My year began with cupcakes to reward my students, experiments to fly paper airplanes and learn the scientific method, a cozy reading nook in the corner of my room for free time and Math Lab on Fridays including games and proficiency practice. It eventually crumbled into dreadfully serious meetings with my principal opening up my contract, untrue accusations that I was not teaching math to my children according to the book and misunderstandings - false rumors - from parents resulting with intimidating letters placed in my mailbox.

I teamed with three 5th grade teachers, and we seemed to hit it off and enjoy working together. We ate lunch together and had team meetings together. We shared ideas and were basically on the same page regarding classroom dynamics and general discipline. We each had our own homerooms, but one teacher taught social studies, one teacher taught language arts, and I taught math. There were never any issues between us, at least none that were spoken to me.

I taught three one-hour classes of 5th grade math to about 75 kids in all. I spent a lot of time over the summer thinking and planning how to make the lessons practical – meaningful - and how the students could be involved as the different math concepts were taught. I didn't want them just playing at their desk, daydreaming or staring out the window. I desperately wanted the kids to be engaged and understand the math since math had sometimes been a struggle for me.

I used the math book to develop packets of guided notes that included vocabulary terms with matching definitions that we matched each day. The packets contained examples from the book that the students did with me while I did them on the board. The intervention specialist took the packets with him to review the math concepts when he took some of his kids out of the room; he said they were very helpful. The packets were a great tool for parents to take home and review with their kids for a test. I offered a math retake on any test if the student scored below a C. Failure just wasn't an option for me.

I made appropriate games about math concepts according to the Ohio State Standards that the kids played to help learn and review current math skills. We played these games in small groups on Fridays in Math Lab. I thoroughly enjoyed working with my aide everyday who was skilled enough to be a teacher herself.

My class and I started out with a great relationship – warm, comfortable and trusting. I had parents coming in to help with Math Lab on Fridays. The principal frequently visited my room in the fall smiling with comments like "everything seems to be going really well for you this year." It was, and I relaxed into an atmosphere of trust between the principal and myself that seemed to be in place. I had finally found my niche, the niche I was trained for.

My class consisted of 25 squirrely 5th graders - some with emotional and behavioral needs; such is the lot of the new teacher. I was excited to meet the kids and be their new teacher. My classroom was designed to be warm, friendly, encouraging and disciplined for those students under my care, and my plans were working well - seemed to be pleasing to all. I consulted heavily with my mentors to make sure things were going smoothly.

Unfortunately, I missed the first week of school with mysterious and severe abominable pains, perhaps a strong reaction to an abrupt, untimely and shocking death of my good friend's husband. When I returned to school the second week, I met my students, and the day began with cupcakes of introduction on their desks which immediately won them over. I laid out the classroom procedures. I explained that I would meet with them at recess if they wanted to have me help them with any problems with fellow classmates on the playground. I had a signup sheet for "eating lunch with Mrs. Carpenter" that was usually full every day but Friday when I would go out with the 5th grade team to a neighborhood restaurant for pizza. I baked cookies, brownies or cupcakes for the kids whenever they filled up our marble jar with 25 marbles for good behavior, compliments from other teachers and substitutes or everyone turning in completed homework on time.

My classroom was thriving and plans were working - until December. But that same mysterious shadow of suspicion from an unknown source was still following me, still surrounding me after I left Title I to enter the 5th grade classroom. I just couldn't fight against something I couldn't see - but it was still there. Eventually, this new, anxious, suspicious principal became its victim resulting in confusion and false perceptions of me. Apparently, someone was alerting this principal to be concerned about me – someone in the darkness who kept their presence a secret, who never brought their concerns to me personally.

By December, the destruction began and things started to fall apart. I was called into my principal's office and accused of not teaching math correctly and just "talking about math" – not teaching it. This was unfounded and confusing. She felt that I was not using the math book. Again - untrue. I think she thought that I was not using the book because of the packets that I had developed. I tried to explain what I was doing and let her look at them but to no avail. It made no sense to me that she would have any concern. I quit doing the math packets as she requested and read from the book alone. The kids missed them.

I was accused of having "inappropriate homework." I had developed ungraded homework with:

conversion problems – inches to feet, pints to gallons, etc.
some achievement review problems
some problems about the current math concepts that we
were studying in class

The homework was explained to the kids every day and corrected; the kids received ten points of credit just for doing it, right or wrong. It was power-packed to help the kids get where they needed to be. I was told not to continue with that homework. I stopped creating those homework sheets as requested - with much disappointment.

The principal opened up my three year contract so she could do weekly observations. She assured me that she had no malicious intent and was not trying to take my job, but just wanted to offer suggestions. That was fine with me because

I had the experience and successful background to feel very confident in what I was doing; I was certainly willing to grow and cooperate with her, but I knew that my students were doing well and gaining in their math knowledge. I just knew it from their test scores, working with my aide and the special education teacher, as well as the correct and confident answers from my students each day in math class.

But the mystery continued. As she pursued this path of concern - doubt and suspicion - my position as the teacher to my 5th grade students and classroom diminished. At times, the principal would ask if I was confused. Other times, she downplayed what I had accomplished in my special education class at the previous school. I knew this was a record someone was playing for her. Mr. Barnes had retired, and she had no contact with him. She said things to me that were just plain false like replaying a record that had come from an unknown source, and it was simply wrong. She wasn't even in the district while I worked at the other school. She had no first-hand knowledge of my work at the other building other than conversations with personnel still in the district. And someone was talking about me and talking a lot.

The only thing that made any sense to me was remembering the warning by my former principal before he retired, and I was glad that I was aware of it. God used that warning and kept me safe from self-doubt and destruction. I had achieved too many successes in 16 years of teaching to buy into this intimidation. I knew what I was doing, and that the kids were thriving.

There were constant, insignificant criticisms:

"Are you teaching math concepts or just talking about them?" This made absolutely no sense to me whatsoever.

She felt that I was spending too much time teaching fractions. I disagreed because I knew that 5th graders needed to understand several harder concepts about fractions to be prepared for 6th grade:

reducing fractions
adding and subtracting like denominators
adding and subtracting unlike denominators
multiplying and dividing fractions
mixed numbers
adding and subtracting mixed numbers
renaming fractions
improper fractions

We were lucky to get through all that instruction in six weeks! I had six years of previous experience in 5th grade to make those decisions and schedules with confidence. I had done this before.

I prayed, "What are you doing, God?"

I tried to honor this principal by doing everything she asked me to. But, she just seemed to question everything happening in my room.

By January, the damage to my classroom was well underway as the students and their parents felt the effects of this negative – suspicious - atmosphere but had no clue as to what was happening to me and to their 5th grade.

One day after school in January, I was called into the office with the other 5th grade teachers and told that they wanted the 5th graders to change back to self-contained classrooms instead of the way we had been working. There were no reasons given except the other teachers apparently wanted to be self-contained. The principal agreed to this change - six weeks before the Ohio Achievement Tests were given in March! I really had no say in the matter. The other teachers had apparently been meeting with the principal, and it had already been decided. I thought, "How foolish to change everything six weeks before their big test." I didn't know what the other teachers had already taught.

I stressed and stressed that weekend trying to gain the knowledge of what had been taught by the other teachers in language arts and social studies during the prior five months. Fortunately, that decision to become self-contained only lasted for one day because of a scheduling conflict with band.

Two parents wrote letters to the principal with their concerns about me. By request, I met with one of them and the principal at parent-teacher conferences in February. The conference was relaxed, smooth and productive. After the conference ended and everyone left, that parent came back into my room and apologized to me.

"I never went into the office to complain about you. Because of the principal's probing, she wanted us to meet. I feel that this has gone way beyond any point of legitimate concern that I carried about you."

I thanked her for her honesty. "Dear God, do You know what's going on here?" I kept wondering. "What *was* going on?"

The other letter came a few weeks later. It was from a parent who had helped me in Math Lab each Friday during the first of the year and had expressed her joy with what was happening in our room and with me. We had a comfortable, warm relationship. We seemed to be on the same page regarding her child. She had no awareness of the difficulty our classroom was enduring and the rumor mill that was apparently running rampart throughout the school. Her letter was extremely condemning and vicious, full of condemnation about my relationship with her child; her child was eventually removed from my class. I just didn't understand any of this. She never came to me with her concerns. I was not a mean, out-of-control teacher at all but cared about my kids. In the past, I was always accepted by my parents and students – a popular, desirable teacher. None of this made any sense:

puzzling
shocking
frustrating
hurtful

disturbing

By February, many of my colleagues in the upper grades became distant, and each day I spent most of my lunches eating by myself in my room with a few of my students. I didn't know who to trust anymore.

"Where was this coming from and why?" I prayed, "I trust You, God."

Even in the midst of all this, I knew that I could still trust my God – the One who had been faithful to me all these years. He must have a plan. I knew that the principal had no control over me - God did; He promised that it was working for my good. Because this made no sense, I knew He was somehow involved in all this. I knew that God had gotten me back into teaching in the first place. I remembered the story of Joseph being sold as a slave in Egypt - but still . . . .

God provided a wonderful Christian friend from our Bible study who became my objective compass to guide me through the rest of this mess.

"You were hired to teach those kids, so teach them. Just do everything that she asks you to do, but keep your eyes on your students and their well-being." And that is just what I did. I also kept my eyes on Jesus and enjoyed teaching math. I never lost my confidence in what I was doing or how I was teaching. I knew good teaching, and I knew what I saw in my classroom. I really rose above it all.

By late February, the weekly concerns and suspicions continued and still made no sense to me. It was like I was in another world – her world verses mine. I was teaching math, my students were learning and there were no problems in my room other than perhaps a sense from the kids that something was amiss. There was some sort of perception problem; some of the things she said just seemed to be misconceptions of her style verses mine. I just didn't know what the problem was.

It was so negative from the office that I seriously considered resigning, but was strongly encouraged by Mr. Barnes, who I called for advice, that resigning could bite me later for future employment. I could actually be put on probation by the state. So, I decided to hang in there with this principal and all the madness.

The next visit to the principal's office offered me an ultimatum, "You need to think about what you want to do next year, because math is not working out for you."

I explained that I was not planning on making any more changes. I knew that the kids understood the math, and I felt that I had been switched around too many times in this district.

By this time, the kids were thriving in my three math classes. They understood percent, negative numbers, mixed numbers, prime numbers, etc. The Star Test results in March revealed that two class averages were at the 6.0 grade level, while the class with the intervention kids was at 5.6. That was amazing! I was *so* happy because they understood most of it, and I had reached my goal. I was very comfortable with the responses, seatwork and assessments that I was receiving back from the kids. Most knew the math really well!

March came and, along with it, the Ohio Achievement Test. As I administered the test, I thought it was very fair and that my kids should be OK. The principal was concerned that an intervention child who she was testing in her office didn't pass the test. Later, I discovered that he *did* pass that test and the 5th grade math results were very satisfactory considering all the pressure and limitation that was placed on me. My class passed the test and, along with the other elementary school, our district's scores came in third in the county behind two other districts that usually came in first – pretty good for my first year under severe duress!

I only wished that I had been given more liberty to meet my students' needs in the method that I had chosen to teach math before I was stopped. Fortunately, I had taught many difficult concepts before I was so abruptly redirected.

Whether it was expectation or rigid management style, in all fairness to me, the administration really did not take much time to analyze and evaluate with an open mind what strategy I was using - it certainly wasn't complicated - before criticizing my math classes and me as an educator that year. In 16 years of instruction, I had never faced anything like this. It was just all plain crazy and beyond my understanding!

After the test was over, I had been told by seasoned teachers in the past that it was OK to "lighten up" and do more "fun stuff" instead of just seatwork and test review. I knew that I had plenty of time to teach the remaining concepts in the book. Thus, I decided and had promised my 75 math students that they would spend a week creating math games with vocabulary terms, problems, answers and critical thinking.

One day as I talked this over with a colleague near the office who liked the idea, the principal overheard me. She immediately called me into her office, closed the door behind me, politely asked me to sit down and declared that I had broken trust with her prescribed agenda; I was not to do the games. I needed to "get back into the book." Again, I didn't realize that creating math games was severely wrong. Didn't we do that stuff in educational classes? I agreed - no problem - and went back to my room thinking that was an end to it.

The next day, I found a sealed letter from the district office in my mailbox. I had received a written reprimand from the superintendent about my straying from the curriculum in reference to the planned games and would be considered for disciplinary actions.

SHOCKING!
HURTFUL!
BETRAYED!
STABBED!

TATTLE-TAILED!
WRITTEN-UP!
WHAT?

My intentions were always honorable and for the kids. I hadn't even *done* the games as the principal commanded, and I still received this reprimand.

And then, another summons to the principal's office. I laughed to myself that I was getting called to the principal's office much more often than I ever did as a child. This was just ridiculous!

I prayed, "Thank You, God, that You are with me in all this, but what are You doing?"

"The superintendent wants to meet with you, tomorrow," informed the principal.

Well, that was just fine with me. It was about time to talk this out, and I expected that we would have a rational discussion about this year and the plans to follow. He knew me and would listen. I had a good relationship with him. He knew of my history with the district. He had always been very positive and knew what an effective and popular teacher I was for the two years under Mr. Barnes in special education. Mr. Barnes had told him I was one of the best that he had ever hired. He had heard the parent compliments. The superintendent, himself, had told me I was doing a "great job" when I worked at the other school. Surely, this meeting would straighten things out in a sensible manner.

The meeting was called. I walked into the superintendent's office and sat down in the chair across from his desk; his back was turned to me. He turned around in his chair as soon as I was seated. I faced a stone-faced superintendent who was operating in full authority – pulling total rank over me. My principal and my union representative were also there.

"Because of your poor performance and parent complaints, we are moving you back to Title I for next year. One of the Title I teachers is willing to trade with you. You should be so thankful. You will be watched and critiqued for your success. But unless there are major turnarounds, we will need to take further disciplinary actions."

I was not prepared for this at all, and I was *certainly* intimidated - I really didn't know what to say. Never – ever – ever - ever had I ever experienced anything like this before! This was certainly not the classroom or school experience that I had ever enjoyed as a former teacher. What had I done so wrong to merit this kind of treatment?

I had no desire to argue or defend myself because it was so:
over-the-top
unbelievable
demoralizing
strange
intimidating
and just plain appalling

Regardless of what anyone else said, I knew that I had done a bang-up job with my 5th grade math students, and they were ready for 6th grade. The whole thing was:
beyond belief
painful
hard to understand
just a mystery
Why ... ?

As I went through this whole ordeal, I kept praying and sought the Lord. I decided if there were any more complaints that I would resign. This seemed impossible to imagine because I had not done *anything* to deserve this kind of treatment. Losing this job appeared just as impossible as getting a teaching job in the first place. I was just numb, but I still enjoyed teaching math to my three classes and, of course, the kids - they were clueless.

I wasn't willing to go through any more hassles trying to please this principal, and I couldn't deal with this shadow that kept following me around. Enough was enough. If they didn't like my teaching and I did than we just couldn't work together. I was not willing to allow my Title I mentor to exchange places with me when she loved her job and was trying to save me. She would not pay the price for my mystery.

"Follow the path and leave the results to me," I remembered and operated in my comforting, God-given thought that was taped to my refrigerator at home in my kitchen.

And then, one day, when I walked in the office after school, I saw another letter in my mailbox - another concern and another parent - one who knew me well and who wanted to meet with her husband, the principal and myself after school to discuss their concerns.

I made up my mind to resign.

We had a relaxed, friendly meeting while I answered their questions about all sorts of misconceptions and false information as the rumor mill outside my room kept working overtime - fast and furious.

"Why does your homeroom have three math classes when the others don't?"

I calmly explained, "Our math class is split in half by recess. Recently, one of the other 5th grade teachers suggested that all three 5th grades do a short ten minute math review first thing in the morning to freshen-up on math terms and skills two weeks before the test."

I don't remember the rest of the concerns, but they were just as meaningless. I really did feel bad for these misinformed parents who would lose a good teacher – one who really did care a whole lot about their kids and their education; I was powerless to change their terrible misconceptions. It was all just so strange.

After I handed in my resignation, the principal stayed out of my room and let me teach my classes in peace and quiet. It was wonderful for me, but many of my students were guarded and knew something was wrong. They couldn't understand why a

God Didn't Have to Make the Crickets Sing

fellow classmate complained and was removed from my class. They tried to explain to her that things were "OK." My students paid a high price because I certainly would not relay anything to them about what was *really* going on.

God had prepared me for this bout by the two wonderful and efficacious years that had preceded me in my special education class with the comments from my former principal, the satisfaction of the parents, the kids' educational progress and the smiles on their faces. I had enjoyed 11 previous years of enjoyable, effective classroom and subbing experience which cushioned this blow. But this was supposed to be *the answer*; this was to be the thing that was supposed to solve all my concerns:

my money
my retirement
my benefits
my career
This was my miracle!

In June, the principal came in to say "good-bye" and tried to smooth things over. She mentioned that this was "very sad."

I just didn't have much to say to her except "This *is* very sad because we both wanted the same thing, success for our students." I had no professional relationship with her. She had managed to lose a caring, conscientious teacher.

She sighed, "Why do you think this year has been so hard?"

I replied, "Because I believe that God is leading me out of here," That was the only thing that made any sense to me and gave me some real peace.

I really had no ill will or antagonism towards her or the district. Jesus Christ was my boss and to Him I was accountable - owed my allegiance. I only knew that I had lost my security, my teaching career, my position for no good reason and that God had allowed it. It was just too weird, strange and unexplainable. I had no idea what He was doing, but He was in control - I did know that. He was still driving the car, but I was numb and very intimidated, now, by school administrators.

As I packed up that June afternoon, I turned and took a last look at my classroom wondering why this had all happened and why my dream had died - before I shut the door. I walked out of the old building to a beautiful and warm, summer day, got in my new Nissan Altima with the sunroof and drove home without looking behind me. I was sure that I did not *ever* want to see either that small town or their school ever again.

I didn't have a clue what my future would look like.

But God did-

Chapter 18

Walking in the Spirit

We live by faith, not by sight. II Corinthians 5:7

It was early June. I was home, and I was an emotional mess. I was very shaken by what had recently happened in my life – trying to connect the dots and solve the missing links of the mystery. I had now lost my future, my plan, and I needed time to heal. I was totally broken and traumatized. I felt confused and timid. I kept reviewing in my mind, "What had I done to deserve this, God? Now what?"

I was empty of dreams, life, purpose and real hope.

I was empty of me and deaf to any song.

Through all our trials, I had always believed my trusty plan - that I could rescue us and get a teaching job to stabilize our lives and our future. It was:

my rock

my hope

my salvation

I had fought – hard – to free us from all the pain and problems that we had faced as a family by trying to make this answer happen. And it seemed like God had agreed – for a while anyway.

But now that plan was gone. Now, I would really have to trust in Him and trust in Him - alone. I had no choice because I had been emptied.

There was no sense even talking about crickets and their songs, anymore, because just about nothing existed for me.

But God was still in control and had allowed a drastic work in my life. God knew that I had some severe spiritual lessons to learn, and they were extremely painful.

How do you walk in the Spirit anyway? He was going to teach me, and I would learn my lessons well. This was to become a great time of healing, encouragement and direction from my Heavenly Father who was still with me and had not left me for one moment, not for one second.

That summer I stayed quiet, rested and healed. My nephew in Virginia died in his early 20's unexpectedly, but I could not make the trip to go to the funeral. I had been through too much, and I was just too exhausted, broken and unstable to face anyone. I really had nothing to offer anyone at that time anyway but hopelessness and quiet desperation.

I requested that my husband and I meet with a dear Christian couple who had basically mentored me through my 5th grade teaching experience from Hell to gain some support and guidance.

"I can't do this," I moaned to them - my flesh, my independent spirit crying out. "I am a responsible person. We need income for the future. We have no:

retirement

pension

substantial savings."

As those words rang out, I remembered saying them one other time in my life during a period of severe testing and darkness when I had to leave my comfortable home in Indiana after the affirmative-action monster devoured my husband's job, and I walked off into great darkness – the great unknown.

God Didn't Have to Make the Crickets Sing

It seemed like there were more monsters consuming my life at every turn instead of blessings, at least, the blessings I was looking for.

I just couldn't see, couldn't feel, couldn't hold onto God any more, couldn't dream – believe. I just existed. I was a responsible person. I needed to work to save my family, provide for our future, provide for me, but that idea was deader than a doornail - just like I was. My heart, life and song were now so silent – immeasurably silent. The words of this page cannot begin to describe my desperation, my emptiness, my death.

I was ready to hear the song.

Jeff's job with the small CPA firm ended after eight years when the company began losing some large accounts. He was looking for employment again. Jeff had a friend who had started a small tax business a few years earlier. During the past year Jeff had been helping him do taxes in his small local office. He made a grand total of $8,000.00 that year! That certainly wouldn't pay our bills and didn't seem too promising, but Jeff didn't seem too engaged or encouraging to me about his ability to find another job or perhaps his desire to even do so. He had been through too much as well. Jeff really felt that the tax business was growing and would provide a promising future for him. I still couldn't see or dream how this situation was *ever* going to provide enough money. It seemed that this was nothing more than blind trust. This didn't seem reasonable or workable, but I was too worn out to care. I had heard that many times faith seems impossible and illogical.

Well, I was there.

I decided that I needed to try to calm my emotions and confusion by doing one important thing. I went to visit the Dean of Continuing Education at the college where I was working to complete my Master's degree in reading. I entered his office to receive a friendly greeting, and we sat down. I spent some time sharing my mystery - with all its hurts and confusion - to a person who held much interest and compassion for me. I asked him if he would look at my math agenda and materials to have him explain what had happened to me, and what I had done wrong.

As he leafed through a packet, he said emphatically, "This is excellent! She was just plain wrong. Don't let this stop you from teaching. Sometimes this kind of thing *does* happen for many strange reasons."

That was easy enough for him to say, but my confidence, ego, dream and stamina were shot. He encouraged me to finish my Master's program, but I just couldn't - for what reason? It seemed so hopeless. It was just too hard, and I was tired - very tired. I had decided not to pursue another special education job at that time – maybe down the road -somehow. But I was dazed and full of fear about anything concerning administrators in education. What if a new district found out what happened? What about another invisible, insidious shadow of destruction following behind me for no reason? People talk, you know, especially in a small town. I felt branded with a solid "D" on my chest – destroyed.

My daughter was pregnant and would need a sitter that fall, so I decided to babysit again. I was looking forward to giving my life some meaning. In my faith and walk with God, I knew the immense importance of being there for my grandkids so they wouldn't have to go to daycare. I knew how influential I could be in sharing my faith and Bible stories with them. I knew that establishing a relationship with them was so important. Could God have removed me from teaching seventy-five 5th graders in public school to be available for my own family's needs and my grandkids? Maybe - maybe, He thought this was more important. It certainly had more eternal consequences.

"Follow the path and leave the results to me."

I also decided that it was not my job to provide or save my family's finances. I had a husband who needed to do that. I had

God Didn't Have to Make the Crickets Sing

seen too much to not know that God was still there with His perfect plan, and that I needed to trust Him like Moses facing the Red Sea – again. I knew He was with Jeff.

I needed to walk in the Spirit. I needed to walk in the dark with the Light of the World in my life – holding His hand. But how?

Again I got professional in what I was doing. My husband and I got our basement all readied-up by purchasing new carpet and fixing and painting some of the paneling. We traded my new Nissan Altima for a new Nissan van that could seat six children. My world had changed.

Two other boys signed up for my childcare and started in August. My 4-month old grandson came in December so by January first, I was watching three boys. This time it felt alright. My answer about teaching was gone, and I was done fighting because I knew God had led me out of that job. This time, I was really following a path and looking to God for His supply.

As I thought about it, I knew this work would help provide the finances we needed. Every day was a regular babysitting day, greeting the excited children and their thankful moms first thing in the morning as they walked in my door.

God challenged me, "Christianity is either true, or it's not true. Make up your mind! And if it is true, then get into the total game and, if not, quit doing church and prayer - the whole thing."

I had more decisions to make.

And then, one day – one precious day, I became aware of more life-changing thoughts from my Heavenly Father:

"Stay in the now."
"Don't analyze."
"Do the task for the day."
"Speak the truth."
Wow! I wrote them down on a small notebook:
"Stay in the now."

"Don't analyze."
"Do the task for the day."
"Speak the truth."

These were God's faithful tools of strength and power in my life. These four principles taught me how to enjoy peace and victory every day. Just like the chicken soup episode back in Marion, I now gained a powerful direction of how to *live* my life. These spiritual tools were *so huge* for me because they taught me how to walk spiritually. They gave me inner strength and power. They kept my focus - a focus on the Lord. They kept me at rest - let Jesus drive the car while I stay in the backseat. God showed me how to focus on my task and think, stand and speak only His truth about circumstances from scripture. He would provide, and I didn't have to rely on my feelings or disappointments. These principles were easy to learn because I was so broken and emptied inside.

I began walking each day with Him, focused on the task that He asked me to do at *that* moment, not with resentment, bitterness or fear, but with a real sense of peace and rest.

I asked myself, "What am I supposed to be doing right now?" I rested my mind, "Don't try to figure out God and His plan. Just do my task."

I realized that I shouldn't waste time speaking my emotions, but instead speak what God says in His word – the truth – the absolute truth about His care of me. "God will provide."

I knew that God was in Control – the theme of my day.

I looked up scriptures about strength and peace and found my key verse:

". . . in quietness and trust is your strength." Isaiah 30:15

I understood that I had never lived my life that way before – never! I was self-reliant and determined to succeed. I had followed all the rules the world said to do. I relied on my own strength.

In a few months when autumn began, God provided another huge piece for healing in my life. I was acquainted with a couple of teachers at my church. As I shared with them what had happened, they were interested and encouraging. I asked them to come over to my house for a visit. They came, and we eventually developed into a weekly Bible study at my house. It just sort of happened, and they gladly participated. They were both teachers, but both were out of the classroom – one retired and the other reason unknown to me.

That began six years of a dynamic, power-packed time of deep, deep spiritual friendship, sharing and healing for all three of us as we met each Wednesday night. Starting at 7:00, we studied books by Watchman Nee:

The Normal Christian Life
Spiritual Authority
Sit, Walk, Stand
The Holy Spirit

with great discussion and insight that would sometimes last until 11:00 or 11:30 at night. I had *never* experienced such deep unity, spiritual power and fun with two believers. It was exhilarating; I just felt so much spiritual strength being fused into my inner being. It provided powerful momentum and satisfying fellowship for healing in all areas of my life that had been out of balance for years. It was just a God-thing, and He accomplished His purpose. Each of us had deep hurts and trials at that time which I did not know anything about – but God did. He brought us all together at that certain time to open us up, to share our pain and to help us recover from some pretty devastating events in all our lives. Not only did we have Bible study, we went out together:

shopping
dining
watching movies
laughing
crying
sharing

> relaxing at a snowy, weekend retreat in a log cabin at the state park

These were truly some of the most profound, giving and caring friendships that I had ever known in my life, and the others felt the same way.

Each year, Jeff kept making monetary gains in his work by doing taxes where it was becoming obvious that this new occupation was steady and profitable for us - a beautiful provision of God. The business kept growing by leaps and bounds. He doubled his salary the next year and saw it increase each year; the little tax company grew substantially to become one of the largest in the county.

My husband worked every Saturday throughout the year either doing taxes or working two evenings at a golf course. Since I was free on Saturday nights, my new-found friends and I found great joy in going out many Saturdays to watch a movie or eat at a restaurant with loads of girl talk and Christian fellowship. We went places where I had never been, places like state park lodges for lunch, shopping at Easton and exploring outlet shops that were nearby. We just had lots of fun and new adventures – a healthy healing for me who had been so bound by fear and disappointment in my rescue attempt. God provided just what I needed for my emotions to heal, and it worked beautifully because a new Gail was emerging out of the darkness – a Gail that was:

> walking in the Spirit
> coming into emotional balance
> giving up control
> following a path
> decorating my home again
> driving on freeways again
> baking sweet treats again
> exercising again
> enjoying my children again

being a girl again
enjoying life again
bonding with my new grandchildren

This Gail would find what she had been looking for – all the love, security and balance that she had been seeking in all the wrong places – not in the world, but in her precious Lord.

He had completed my music for me, and I was ready to hear it any day; the story of a new transformation of my life in Christ was still developing, and I would be set free.

Chapter 19

The Reading Curriculum

As my new life unfolded, and I began babysitting again, three passions still remained in my heart:

helping struggling readers

teaching reading by decoding or phonics

selling my stories that I wrote for my transitional 1st graders when I was teaching Title I reading two years ago

One day in June, I called my Christian friend who had been such a guide and encouragement to me as I faced my recent ordeal. I began discussing my work, my disappointments and what to do. She said, "Finish the stories whether you ever use them again or not."

That was good advice. It gave direction and peace to my heart, a meaning and a purpose to all the madness that had just recently happened to me. My extremely successful experience with reading instruction in both that DH class and with the Title I reading students in transitional 1st grade along with private tutoring of several failing readers convinced me that God had given me those story lessons for a reason and that they would help many kids. I really cared about building reading success.

There was much talk everywhere about students failing reading and dropping out; I had seen some of the problems firsthand in my district. The newspapers were writing about it. The talk shows were talking about it, and the states were coming down hard with more testing and threats of failing students who did not pass the 3rd grade state reading tests. Teachers were being required to become "Highly Qualified" and encouraged to get more classwork by earning a Master's degree.

Teaching reading had become a huge moral issue for me. My experience showed me that many kids were failing and didn't seem to gain the reading abilities which they could have achieved. They were just being sent through the system. Schools didn't seem to be teaching with phonetic decoding for unknown words as a primary strategy but encouraging the readers to memorize lists of words, look at pictures, look at initial consonants or just plain "guess" to figure out what the words were from the context of the sentence. This wasn't reading to me. There was no real emphasis on word families in unknown words to build reading skills through decoding. That is why I had written the stories for my students in the first place.

I loved my little story lessons from my Title I class:
they were focused
they were repetitive
they were systematic
they were short and simple
they were supportive
they showed what the reader's problem was
they coordinated spelling and writing using one word family
they were kid-friendly

A strange passion had taken over my heart which I never experienced while teaching 5th grade.

When I resigned, I had not finished the stories that I had written for my Title I students. I had only written one book of 17 short vowel stories and half of the stories in the next long vowel book. I had quit writing these story lessons when I transferred to 5th grade. I knew the story lessons were good and had seen their success with my six 1st graders. I had seen the kids' confidence build and the smiles return to their faces. I knew these lessons would be useful to help many kids learn how to read.

"Finish the stories whether you ever use them or not." That became my driving purpose – my goal.

So I began writing. I developed the approach of memorizing one word family a week and a few high-frequency words. The next week, I added another word family, more high-frequency words and reviewed the previous ones. The story lessons supported words from the word family that were being taught as well as writing words with that word family. Then the children could spell the words on their own instead of just memorizing external spelling lists that had no phonetic pattern. Common sense asked, "Would it be easier to know the sound of 'oi' in 'spoil' and blend the word or just memorize all these words?"

spoil
moist
boisterous
pointer
joined
exploit
Detroit

The answer was obvious - decoding was much easier and allowed the reader to read so many more words of that family instead of forcing him to memorize whole lists of words with no patterns that were used in sentences. This knowledge of word families and decoding was especially easier for struggling readers.

As I became more involved in finishing this project, I began to wonder if maybe there was something more – maybe my path had just changed, and God had given me a new mission.

God Didn't Have to Make the Crickets Sing

In quiet places late at night or on the weekends, I began writing lists. I could see patterns, story lines and plots in my lists. I would make lists of words containing a certain word family on a piece of paper. It seemed like I was able to see a story immediately from certain groups of words.

Many of the stories came to me first thing in the morning or late at night when I was lying in bed and quiet. The stories just seemed to flow right out of me, and I knew that God was inspiring me – involved in this. Sometimes, I had to literally leap out of bed to grab a pencil as the story flowed out of my mind onto a sheet of paper while I watched my hand fly across the page writing the words of the story. I started keeping a tablet next to my bed. Most of "There is Thunk" was written like this. It was effortless and most gratifying.

I became totally engaged in this project, sorting, organizing and categorizing high-frequency words, making flashcards of word families and structuring the story lessons – quite a daunting task. I went to work typing, editing, cutting, pasting and drawing illustrations. God had to be in this because it was almost effortless, effortless from the format for the story lessons to the stories themselves. There was no struggle with this work – no long hours racking my brain trying to think of a character or story line, trying to get something down on paper. I realized that to assign someone a thesis project of "write a reading curriculum" would prove to be a formidable task and over-encompassing if the author had to just think it up.

But this was different. This project would certainly need to be heartfelt – inspired. It flowed out of me - so easily, so methodically and so beautifully. Where all this guidance and knowledge came from was certainly not mine, but guided by a Heavenly Hand - it *had* to be and certainly was a gift. The format and method of the curriculum was impressive and extremely effective in its approach and usability. I loved the books with their story lessons, and my readers did too.

It took the rest of the year to finish the Level B book of long vowels, and the Level C book with diagraphs, diphthongs, etc. Then, I knew that I needed to write *Syllabication* to teach the sounds of blends, endings, prefixes and suffixes in multisyllabic words to finish the job. Instead of complicated, boring worksheets or texts, I wrote lists of words with common prefixes or suffixes to read and reread. This method allowed the student to hear what the prefix or suffix actually sounded like and to provide practice in reading multisyllable words. This method made much more sense to me than what I had previously seen in other reading curriculums.

By spring, I had finished the stories and created a reading curriculum of nine pieces. A friend helped me edit, proofread and check for any errors. It needed very little changing. I named it *Carpenter Phonics* and my son-in-law created a website. It was all very-exciting!!

Now, I needed to be validated. To get another opinion and some endorsement, I called a professor from a previous reading class while I was pursuing my Master's degree in college.

I found the number and dialed. "Hi, it's Gail Carpenter, one of your former students. I have written a reading curriculum that I think is pretty good, and I wondered if you would meet with me to give me your opinion." I held my breath.

"I would be delighted," she replied. "I'll meet you at Wendy's."

Overcoming my recent past and fearful experiences of threatening shadows with administrators, I packed up the books and met with her at Wendy's. "This is a really nice program of systematic, controlled, vocabulary instruction," she remarked as she leafed through the books. "It's definitely a piece in good reading instruction."

Yes!! Yes!! Yes!! Her endorsement did a lot to encourage me and insured me that I knew what I was doing.

My Bible study with my two new and close friends continued to meet on Wednesday nights. One of the gals was a retired 1st grade teacher. While I had been telling the group about what I was doing and asking for prayer, she became curious, "I'd like to see what you're doing."

The next day I packed up the books and drove over to her condo. "These are great! Oh, if I had only had something like this when I was teaching 1st grade. I'd like to write you an endorsement," another great encouragement!

By this time I felt very comfortable with this new curriculum because I knew:

I liked it

my professor liked it

my friend, the retired teacher, liked it

that the first book had worked when I was teaching Title
    I reading

I was really pleased at the progress that I had made with my curriculum and the feedback that I had received from some colleagues who would be able to judge it – so far so good. I dreamed of using these books to teach children how to read, but I knew that I had only finished the first book and only a few lessons of the second when I was teaching. Would the whole curriculum really work to help someone learn to become a successful reader? I still didn't know.

God knew that I needed some students to read through the whole program - a test group. Then I would feel more comfortable introducing this - more confident.

As I went about my days babysitting, I trusted God with this mission and kept my focus on Him. One evening the telephone rang. I picked up the wireless and answered it. "Hi, my name is Annie Jones. My son, Carl, is having real difficulty in school and needs a reading tutor. I got your name from the teachers' store downtown. Could you please help us? We're desperate, and he's failing reading at school," she asked hopefully.

There it was! God had faithfully provided more direction on the path to meet this need of a "test case" so I would be knowledgeable in moving this curriculum forward.

Carl, his mother and I met for private tutoring for two and a half years in my home. He was dyslexic and had struggled since kindergarten. He was known as a failing reader at school and no one seemed to know exactly what to do to help him. He was defeated, frustrated and hated anything to do with reading. I had seen that before. His parents were concerned and frustrated as well. His mother had experienced reading issues when she was in school and did not want that for Carl. As we continued our tutoring, we worked through the books. He began making significant progress. However, he needed time to finish the program before he would have all the word families that he needed to be a successful reader. The school was still very concerned.

A meeting was called by the school, and I was asked by Carl's mother to meet with his parents, teacher and administrator to discuss Carl's reading concerns. By this time, the parents could definitely see progress, and we encouraged the school not to fail him but to give him a chance to let this curriculum work. He did have some reading issues that severely hindered his progress, but with the strategy of this program I knew that he would make steady progress with his reading – I had seen it before. He still needed time to work through all the families in the three books. The school gave him that chance, and he was not failed. By the time tutoring was over, everyone noticed the remarkable progress that he had made and that he was reading on grade level.

So now I knew that my curriculum worked. The parents, teachers and administrators were all telling *me*. It worked and, not only did it work, it worked really well. I knew that it could be used to help lots of failing or beginning readers – a noble purpose, and one which I was passionate about.

But how?

What a huge mountain to climb; I would have to deal with:

schools

administrators

teachers

competitors

publishers

I kept my focus on God.

Shortly after Carl had finished coming to my house for tutoring, God moved again with another direction in my path. One day Jeff came home from work and said, "I was talking to someone at work who's concerned about her son in kindergarten and his reading. Can you help her? I told her to call you."

Then, another phone call, "Gail, I heard from the church that you help struggling readers. My grandson is failing. Can you help?"

Then, still another phone call, "Gail, I got your name from Carl's mom. My daughter is dyslexic and has struggled with reading ever since kindergarten. She is failing, and we're in crisis. We just don't know what to do. Can you help us?"

And within a month, a wonderful reading group was established for two and a half years at my home to help these three failing readers gain effective reading skills. God had provided another opportunity for me to take struggling readers through the complete reading curriculum and for all of us to see the results.

At the end of two and a half years, not only were the results successful, but they were wonderful - exciting! Everyone saw it:

the parents

the administrators

the reading teachers

the classroom teachers

the students themselves

and me

Not one of my readers tutored in this program failed in their respective schools. By learning word families and stories that supported those families, my three readers ended up strong and confident with successful reading skills.

"You were a God-send!"

"I don't know what we would have done without you!"

"Thank you!"

I began hearing these comments over and over from relieved and thankful parents.

I heard these statements when I taught DH with my nine students. I heard them in my Title I reading. I heard them again from the parents of my tutored students. My background was not teaching reading; it was seven years in 5th grade. I knew that I couldn't take credit for this alone, and I knew that I had been given a gift – a gift inspired by God, and one that was extremely satisfying for me and highly effective in helping kids read.

Again, God was affirming to me this vision, this curriculum and this hope that I could help lots of kids who were struggling or starting their reading journey. Hopefully, this systematic, repetitive method would alleviate some of the confusion and discouragement being experienced by parents, teachers and students. I began thinking and hoping that this may be one of the good reasons why I needed to resign my job at my school - for no good reason.

God says in His word, ". . . in all things God works for the good . . . . Romans 8:28

That seemed to be happening.

"Follow the path and leave the results to me." That is exactly what I was doing, and I was very hopeful in this plan. I was learning to walk in the Spirit, learning to walk as Moses did in the desert, as Paul did on his journey, with my focus on God and trusting in His leading in my life.

Yes, I was ready to hear the song. The crickets were warming up to sing my melody. And this time I would hear it and hear it in overpowering tones.

But there was more to do. The next big step was to visit some of the local schools, preschools and Head Starts in the county. Again, shaking off my fear and intimidation, I decided to walk into the small charter school in town that had been in existence for many years. Here I was, going into a principal's office. I was surrounded by memories of unreasonable visits to my former principal's office. Recently, my experiences in there had done its damage to my emotions.

As I walked into the office, the principal greeted me with a great smile and offered her hand of welcome and interest. "That was a pleasant change," I thought to myself.

I smiled with my bag of books on my shoulder. "I've written a reading curriculum that seems to be very successful with struggling or beginning readers. I wondered if you might take a look and be interested in using it in your school." I explained.

In a warm, friendly atmosphere, she invited me to sit down. I placed the books on her desk and explained the program, explained my passion to help struggling and beginning readers and explained my experience trying to change some mind-sets about using decoding as a primary strategy for effective reading instruction.

She was very interested as she carefully leafed through the pages of the books while I guided her through the format of the lessons. She was impressed. She purchased six sets! Again, this was over-the-top for me, exciting and more enticement to keep following this path – God's path.

"Follow the path and leave the results to me." I recited it many times on my journey.

In the next few weeks, I visited other schools, preschools and educational service centers in the area. One of the ESC directors said, "This is excellent" and bought a set. Most of the rest of the institutions I visited purchased the program - one of those being a local public school.

One day in the grocery store, I ran into an old friend of mine who was homeschooling her children. We began talking, and I told her about the reading curriculum. She was very interested and wanted to buy the books. "I just can't find anything that does the whole job for me. The books are either too easy or don't emphasize decoding." I sold her the books at cost, and she began using the first book. She reported back in a week and was absolutely thrilled with the results of the lessons. She said her daughter loved the lessons and had "taken off" with words and word families. She encouraged me to get involved in the homeschoolers convention coming up in Columbus, Ohio that summer in June. "You should do really well. I'll be praying for you."

I decided to do it. I registered as a vendor and drove off to Columbus, Ohio that June with the curriculum in my car to spend two days at their convention. Several moms came over to discuss and look at the new materials. I was full of passion. Suddenly, as I relaxed for a moment, I saw one mom literally run up to my table.

"I need help with my 7-year old. He can't read. What do you have here?"

I explained:

the curriculum

the rationale

my experience

She bought the whole set and within two years, Ben was reading and doing "just fine." She wrote me a letter saying "I love it, I love it, I love it. It's the only thing that worked!"

This whole reading journey was starting to become very important to me as I could see God guiding and showing me the need for better reading curriculum and the difference it made for our kids.

I now had enough confidence to actually begin making calls to sell the curriculum to schools, and I was passionate to do so. In the fall, I began calling more school districts and preschools in some select locations around central Ohio. A few district curriculum directors bought it - sight unseen - over the phone. I was amazed! One curriculum director bought three sets.

I began receiving excellent feedback from the instructors and parents who were using *Carpenter Phonics*. And I was seeing the results myself as I continued tutoring children at my house who had pretty severe reading problems.

One of the first calls I made was to a national Christian television network to ask how to appear on their program. The person answering said, "Oh, is this about a reading curriculum? I want to buy it -the whole thing!" Amazing, God, and so encouraging!

Sales began totaling $29,000.00!

As I continued to talk to schools and parents, I was beginning to see a huge need for someone with a voice and a curriculum that would help kids gain successful reading skills in a simple, focused method involving word families. I was starting to feel like I was the person – called - to lead many captives free from a system of reading instruction that was failing many children, frustrating many parents and teachers - allowing many kids to feel stupid - and be sent through the system without ever learning to read.

I entered a few conferences:
ESL
homeschool
educators
preschool
Columbus City Schools COTA DAY

And I had successful results and sales. I was receiving positive feedback from teachers who viewed my product:

"This makes so much sense."

"You've really hit reading in the jugular."
"I'm buying this with my own money."
"This program will help me know what to do with my kids in my classroom."
"I don't have the materials needed to help my students advance."
"Can you come and talk to my school?"
"Your price is too low for the quality of this curriculum."

At the suggestion of a teacher of one of the children who I was tutoring, I contacted the curriculum director of the catholic schools in Central Ohio. She was interested in what I was doing, and we met with a 1st grade teacher. She stated, "I think that you have a good program here." She encouraged me to contact some of the catholic schools in her diocese. I did and sold eight sets to the schools.

The second year, I continued my journey. At the suggestion of my husband, I called 11 superintendents from southern Ohio. They set up a meeting, and I addressed them concerning my passion to help kids and the curriculum that I had developed to help reach that goal. I also contacted five districts in Florida and New Mexico because those states were listed as some of the lowest in the nation in reading scores.

But I began hearing the same comment "You need to have data. By law, we have to use researched-based curriculum so send us your data."

data

data

data

How is that supposed to happen?

But God kept me moving me down the path.

"Follow the path and leave the results to me."

One afternoon, the telephone rang. It was a phone call from my Christian friend who had supported me through my trial. "Gail, we just got our newsletter from The Ohio State University, and they are looking for curriculum to research in reading! You should contact them."

Here it was again - my faithful God - His guidance, His provision and path. Wow! This was just too much and very exciting.

I immediately picked up the phone, looked up the number and dialed the university's research department. The secretary to the Director of Research for the university answered the phone in a pleasant voice, "Hello, research department."

I was moving on to the next level of God's path . . . .

Chapter 20

Carpenter Literacy

I had been given a wonderful gift, and now I had been given a requirement - data – to validate its effectiveness to public schools. I was extremely excited about the possibility of working with the university and what it might mean to help me move this curriculum forward.

Stay in the now.
Do the task for the day.
Speak the truth.
Don't analyze.

I had learned to operate in God's four steps enough that I had great peace. But this was exciting - very exciting!

I began explaining, "Hi, my name is Gail Carpenter. I am a certified teacher, and I have written a reading curriculum. I understand that you are looking for items to research in reading, and I wondered if you would take a look at my program."

I explained:
the format
the rationale for the program
my experience with special education
my successes with failing students

my success with the curriculum

"Oh, yes. Can you send us your manuscripts, and we'll get back with you?" replied the pleasant person on the other end of the phone.

"Wow! Bingo!" I thought.

I hung up the phone. I immediately dashed around grabbing the curriculum, carefully packaging it up and sending it off to The Ohio State University.

A few weeks later, I called again to see if the people involved had a chance to examine the books. "Hi, it's Gail Carpenter calling. I was checking in to see if you had a chance to look at the reading materials that I recently sent?" I held my breath, closed my eyes and crossed my fingers.

"Gail, oh, yes, we did. The staff really liked what they saw and would like to set up a meeting with you to discuss your method and experience with the curriculum," replied the secretary enthusiastically. She continued, "This could be huge! If the university researches it, the results of the study will be published in the periodical concerning the data and effectiveness in reading instruction."

Data! There was that word again. I dreamed about this collaboration helping me move to the next level, and I was excited – really excited and encouraged. "Thank you, God, for leading me on this fabulous journey," I prayed. "I've come so far."

"Follow the path and leave the results to Me." The tattered note was still hanging on my refrigerator door held up by a magnet.

The meeting was set up for early summer, and I was on *cloud nine*! This was just too much! Thank you, God. The day finally came, and I jumped into the car happily driving to Ohio State. I parked the car at the Early Childhood Center, plopped the bag that contained the program on my shoulder and traveled up the elevator full of anticipation - also a bit nervous.

What would they say? What would they do? How would they help this curriculum get to those students who needed it? Would the university support me? Could I really help make a change in the dynamics of reading instruction in public schools?

I really wanted to discuss the method of teaching word families and using decoding as an effective reading strategy with any administrator, teacher, parent and student - anyone who would listen - because of the results that I had seen with my young or failing readers. I wanted to convince everyone that reading instruction should look different than just memorizing words and that the knowledge of word families for decoding unknown words was a "gift" to give to anyone learning how to read – like learning the notes of music before you play a song.

I entered the elevator, arrived at the second floor and was escorted into a small office. I was warmly greeted by two department heads:

the Head of Research

the Head of Special Education

and a secretary, Helen, the one I had talked to on the phone.

I began by showing them a video that I had recorded of two 5-year old boys in my preschool reading Book B with me at my house. Even though the video was quite entertaining with the boys' wiggles, giggles and antics, they were definitely reading and decoding. These boys had not entered kindergarten yet.

"How old are those boys?" the Head of Research asked.

"Five," I replied revealing my passion.

When the video was through, we talked about the program briefly. No corrections or concerns were expressed by Ohio State concerning the format, layout or theory of the program. The discussion consisted of:

"We feel that you have a strong program here."

"We would suggest that you change the name from *Carpenter Phonics* to *Carpenter Literacy* since it incorporates much more than just phonics."

"We would like to have you write a teacher's manual."
"We would like you to think about collecting formal data."
"We would like you to incorporate a pronunciation guide in your manual for word families.

The last point surprised me. "Really? You mean there are people who don't know the families?"

"You would be surprised," they flatly stated.

Our meeting lasted two hours – two whole hours! The secretary explained that it was a very good sign.

When I left the building and drove home, I thought about their suggestions. The idea of writing a teacher's manual seemed daunting to me, sort of like someone coming up to you and asking you to write a thirteen component reading curriculum.

When I got home, I glanced briefly at a couple of prepared manuals and prayed, but as God moved, I easily spent the summer writing a simple, teacher-friendly and concise teacher's manual - effortlessly. The format just came to me:

rationale
objectives
preparation
materials needed
implementation
assessments

When I had finished the manual, the thought popped into my head that I needed a Scope and Sequence. "I'm not even sure what that is." I checked some other sources and discovered that I should have one. Again, God was involved in an overwhelming task that turned out to be enjoyable - effortless. I spent my days writing and loving everything that was written down on my paper.

Data, data, they wanted data. I knew I needed data, so I decided to ask a local childcare to participate in a pilot study for the year 2009-2010. The director enthusiastically agreed, and two teachers were on board. One teacher had children ages three and four, and the other pre-k teacher had children ages four and five. I met with the teachers in August to explain the dynamics of the curriculum. I got both teachers started with a few weekly visits.

Within ten weeks, 82% of the kids - ages three through five from both classrooms - knew at least 23 letters and sounds of the alphabet. I also gave a Dibels test to the 5-year old children in May and my own assessments with my program. Several children in the pre-k class scored at a 1st grade level on the Dibels Nonsense Word Fluency and Oral Reading Fluency tests.

Both teachers wrote very favorable reviews of the program. The pre-k teacher told me the children were "upset" when June came, and they didn't get to finish Book B. One of the children asked his dad to buy Book C for Christmas since he wouldn't get to finish it before kindergarten. That was really rewarding to me – a reading curriculum for Christmas!

I hardly had time to think about what had happened back at my school. All of this was going on, and I was immersed in this curriculum. I believed that God had shown me the path to follow and that the results were helping a lot of kids. I was feeling:

very blessed
very busy
very fulfilled
very excited
very free

The next June, I went back to Ohio State again with my wonderful data that I had collected from the childcare. I met with the same people in the same room. I enthusiastically showed them the results that I had collected the previous May, fully expecting rave reviews from them both.

"This is impressive, but you need to use standardized testing, and you really need to get this into school-age classrooms if that is where you want to market your curriculum," they patiently explained. They were still very encouraging with the results that I had, and what I was doing.

But the wind was knocked out of my sails as I drove home. With feelings of discouragement and frustration overwhelming me, I talked to Jesus. "Whoa, how was that *ever* going to happen?

I knew that I had been given something good, but trying to convince schools to get involved seemed hard –really hard. Would a school just let me use them for a study?" I wondered. That idea *did* seem impossible. It seemed like this process was going to take forever. But God kept graciously moving me forward and encouraging me.

In the middle of August, I called two public schools. I got nowhere with the principal of one school and the curriculum director of the other after discussing my need for a pilot study under the direction of Ohio State. They both replied, "We just started using something else, and we really can't ask our teachers to switch right now - maybe another time."

Great - more time and more frustration. But I knew that God was in this with me.

What to do? What to do?

I decided to call some Catholic schools. I called the first one on the list - an inner city ESL school that bought the program a year before.

"Hi, it's Gail Carpenter calling. I'm the author of the reading curriculum that you purchased last year. I am looking for a school that might be interested in participating in a pilot study with kindergarten and 1st grade using the program. I'll donate the materials and collect formal data using Dibels. Would you be interested?"

Their principal was new, but I heard, "I'll have to check with the teachers, but yes, I think so. The Title I children using your program have done very well."

Oh, I was glad, so glad. God just kept me moving along His straight path. I just had to keep following. I was just becoming so aware that He was guiding my life and not *my* prescribed American dream that I had to accomplish and force on my own. He was making some dreams come true, and they really were His dreams being fulfilled in me. Being involved with helping children read with this program was something I loved and enjoyed; I was very aware that my eyes had to stay on Him to fulfill this adventure.

The phone rang the next day, and we set up a meeting a few days before school started with the 1st grade and kindergarten teachers. Again, I packed up the books, drove to the school and watched more dreams coming true. The teachers were on board - one excited, one hesitant – but the principal was supportive and a believer in a phonetic, decoding approach.

After school began, I traveled to the school two days a week for six weeks to get them off to a successful start and fix any concerns or kinks in the curriculum. Everything went smoothly with both teachers doing an amazing job teaching the curriculum for the year. The 1st grade teacher had concerns about collecting grades, so I wrote:

journal entries

workbook pages

short weekly assessments about the stories

high-frequency word assessments that were included with the weekly spelling test

More writing for me during the year and, yet, more inspiration was flowing onto the pages. Again, the format and rationale of these new pieces were needed to help a classroom teacher evaluate her students' daily progress. I was just amazed the amount of pages – the writing – that was occurring in this curriculum. It truly was swelling up inside me. I never could have just sat down and done all this without being inspired, and I knew it - I praised God for it.

That first year in January, I tested 1st grade with Dibels Oral Fluency Assessment. Only five kids hit the target of 40 words a minute. By June, only five kids did *not* hit the target - 80% of the readers passed! I was happy because there were good reasons why the five didn't pass.

The assessments from the books showed us exactly where to put anyone still struggling. The five at-risk children were identified and placed back to review some families before they moved on in the program.

Most of the kindergarten children finished Book A. That meant they could blend short vowel words and know 86 high-frequency words. By finishing Book A in kindergarten, 1st grade could complete the rest of the program by the beginning of 2nd grade. Again great news and progress!

After the second year of using *Carpenter Literacy*, 100% of the 1st graders who began in kindergarten and finished the program passed the Dibels' target score of 40 words a minute. Everyone in 2nd grade made progress.

Research continued into the third year:
Dibels and Woodcock Passage Testing
writing a comprehension book
helping children learn to read.

By 3rd grade, 95% of the kids who began *Carpenter Literacy* in 1st grade were at or above grade level by May 2013. This data brought me great satisfaction!

The study continued for three years, collecting data to prove the effectiveness of *Carpenter Literacy*. For four years, I had annual meetings with the two department heads at Ohio State in June. Discussions with Ohio State included:

"Your program is better than 90% of the stuff out there."
"Working with state legislatures is a good idea for change."
"There is a lot of competition for reading curriculum in
    grades 1-3."
"Where do you see your program being used?"
"Preschool and kindergarten is a high-interest area."
"Sounds like your kids are making a lot of progress."

> "There is much frustration at times about reading instruction in public schools."

I entertained thoughts of helping many children, of discussing the importance of teaching word families for decoding, of challenging current methods of reading instruction on national TV programs or radio talk shows. Only God knows the final result of this wonderful adventure that I've been on, but this gift has already helped many beginning and failing readers become successful, and now a few public schools in my area are beginning to take a serious look.

Chapter 21

My Song

One peaceful evening during this exciting time in my life, I went outside to relax after dinner to enjoy the ending of another busy day. I closed the screen door, walked over to my favorite chair and plopped down - tired. I propped up my feet on the stool at the base of the chair, leaned my head back, closed my eyes and began to relax. As I sat there, I heard something - a powerful song swelling towards me - a rhapsody of harmonious notes, soft melodies swirling around the trees. Sweet tones were traveling from the woods through my backyard to my chair where I sat awakened to this lovely music bombarding my ears with wonder, strength and beautiful love. I knew this song was for me – somehow; I just knew it. Crickets in the woods were singing to me, and I heard their melody loud and clear - I finally heard the song. It penetrated my heart with love. It was so *loud* that it overtook the stillness of the evening in waves of melody playing over and over again. And the musicians were insects – ugly, tiny, black insects - insects created by God with the ability to sing for my pleasure in harmonious tunes.

How could I have missed it for so long? I had been listening to the wrong stanzas – the stanzas of the world - the stanzas of the empty promises that life tempts us with every day - truly the wrong music. The meaning of this song all made sense to me, now – God loved me and was in control. I understood that the cricket chorus had been playing everywhere all my life from my unexpected birth to my present moment. God revealed so much of His notes of love and faithfulness to me that night, notes explaining His presence in my life. I realized that my Creator was saying:

I love you.

I'm here.

I know.

I care about it all.

I have never left you.

I am in control.

I don't know why this time the song grabbed me in such a powerful way - but it did, and I fell into deep worship and thankfulness as the crickets continued to play - my heart swelled with love. I just closed my eyes to enjoy the personal communion from my God to me. I thought about all those years, past years, when crickets were singing all around me, and I just didn't hear:

- the notes of protection for me with a loving mom and dad who had me at 41 when their family was almost grown and gone
- the notes of rescue from several job changes
- the notes of a loving, happy family
- the notes of safety in emotionally dire circumstances from the world
- the notes of wonderful green pastures for times of healing and restoration
- the notes singing about God's never-ending, faithful care through more plant closings and job changes

His melody was everywhere, and I was at peace when I finally heard it.

They were notes removing:

my insecurities
my fears
my pride
my despair
my independence

I just sat there for the longest time and listened. It was such a powerful revelation that night and so simple. I knew that God was speaking to me. In spite of the heat and humidity, those crickets were always singing as a chorus in perfect harmony, not for them, but for me – singing about God's creation - stable, lovely and under His tender care. And I was part of that care, a special object of His love and attention just as we all are.

I was:
protected
adored
provided for
safe

and I was listening - listening intently - and it was soothing and precious. From that moment on when something happened, I heard the song.

Chapter 22

The Photo

In the next couple of years, God began revealing to me sources of genuine pain in my life. Many times, I experienced deeply painful and intense emotional reactions to just ordinary, pleasant experiences in life, especially with relationships. I had a lot of hurt in my life, and I really didn't understand it. I *was* privileged, loved and protected by my parents and family. Why all this pain?

One evening as I was looking through some old photos, I found a picture of my brother and sister with my parents standing on a beach in Florida. My sister was 17 and my brother was 12. Everyone was wearing bathing suits and standing together on the beach - smiling. They all looked so very happy. Suddenly, it hit me and hit me hard – this photo was taken two years before I was conceived, and no one had a *clue* that there would be another child, a little girl - me - in that family.

I looked at my mom with her family and was shocked and thankful that she didn't abort me. Looking at the picture, I so loved and appreciated her for her loving, moral decision. I also understood her shock and pain when she found out she was pregnant. Gracious! Her family was almost raised and here she was being asked to start all over again - with me. I understood the terrible emotional adjustment this pregnancy had to be for her. I'm sure my mother's reaction was difficult and uncomfortable. This pregnancy was not your typical excitement for a baby. This pregnancy was strange, unexpected and interruptive in an already established and happy family. I was certainly a surprise that caused, perhaps, a time of mixed reactions – especially for my dear mom.

My parents were wonderful, but they had to adapt to this "news" in their early 40's of starting again as new parents with a crying baby on their hands. Because of the timing of my birth into my parents' busy lives, I probably spent more time alone and with recommended babysitters then most young children. My grandparents were just too far away and too old to ever establish a warm relationship with me.

Even though I was loved, I felt left out so many, many times as I watched my parents go to parties or sit laughing and visiting with friends while I had to go to bed. I dreamed of the other families with young children as I watched them go places and seem to have so much fun. Again, I felt left out. Lies began growing in my head by the enemy that I was missing out and would never really be wanted or accepted by someone or find happiness. Life seemed to be happening for everyone else.

I was rather shy, wasn't extremely popular in high school - didn't date much. I had a lot of friends but suffered under the usual torment of a typical high school teenager with all the false fantasies that go along with that stage in life. I believed there would be a boy who would fall madly in love with me and rescue me from all my loneliness and feelings of rejection, but deep inside I worried that I would never find him. I wondered if anyone my age would really care and want to spend quality time with me. I felt a huge hole in my heart anxiously looking for this someone and not realizing that the Someone was God Himself.

Once I understood my pain, I was able to deal with it. Through this photo, I knew where my pain came from. It was never intentional, of course, but it was there. I understood many things looking at that photo:

> I understood the loving decision and adjustment of my mother for me.
> I understood why I felt left out and lonely as an only child fitting into my parents' life-style with their other interests in their 40's.
> I understood my longings for a close-knit family.
> I understood that people could not meet my deepest needs.
> I understood that God had always been there for me.
> I understood that He was in control.
> I understood that I could trust Him.
> I understood that I needed to renew my mind and find my emotional needs in God.

Through the past years of blessing and loneliness, disappointment, despair and suffering – my wanderings in the wilderness - I kept believing that success, pleasures and parties were the normal fulfillments of life. And yet, I watched many of those worldly pursuits only turned around to bite the soul of peoples' lives who pursued them. They did not do the trick. They did not:

> bring inner peace
> bring a sense of purpose
> bring excitement that lasts
> bring fulfillment of the heart's deepest needs
> bring an inner warmth of love
> bring hope

As I watched people over the years whose lives I envied so much, I saw many of their lives crash when the parties or careers ended:

> divorce
> mental illness

depression
no hope
disease
emptiness
suicide

The lie of life had been revealed to me. I had always been loved, and everyone did the best that they could do.

As each note of *my* stability was removed from *my* song:
career paths
family
money

God began replacing them with a deep relationship and awareness of His strong arm never letting me go through all the years. He was the Lord of each of my days. I had learned to stay in the back seat and let Him drive my car. He would never fail to satisfy me emotionally and meet all my needs. He loved and accepted me. I had so much to look forward to being with Him. He provided jobs when I needed them, income for our ample supply and emotional healing of His love and encouraging presence in my life day by day. He also gave me four points that helped me reach victorious living:

Stay in the now.
Do the task for the day.
Don't analyze.
Speak the truth.

I began to *really* believe that this Jesus was in control of my life and the Person I would meet someday to thank and worship. He became my best Friend.

The pain of relationships was diminishing as I learned how to love others with agape love. I could now give back to others without expecting them to meet all my needs. The pain was almost gone.

I knew people were blessings – huge blessings – in my life, but my life was created, loved and maintained by God.

My cricket melody was created just for me through a path of frustration, brokenness, disappointment and pain over the years. It was God writing each note deep inside my heart and using all the pain, so I could hear my symphony in time. Truly, the path of suffering and brokenness were His best tools – those deep notes of the song. Through it, I got to know my precious Lord Jesus.

He was now enough. No American dream would ever satisfy now because I had learned to be content in His love and care of me. My focus was now on Him:

not myself
not others
not my opinions
not others' opinions
not "what ifs"
not worldly events
not problems
not jobs

Why do the crickets sing at night? They sing of God's love for me, and I have never forgotten their song.

Chapter 23

Your Song

Have you found a cricket in the corner of your house? Did he live or was he destroyed never to be allowed to play his melody again? My cricket behind my door was set free to rejoin his companions and continue to sing his song. At the time, I didn't realize that he would return to sing for me - but he did - and he truly demonstrated the faithfulness of God for all His creation - for me.

Now, when I go to bed at night in the summer with my window open, I can hear those little critters singing their hearts out in the woods. I find such a joy and peace that God designed them with the ability to chirp their beautiful melodies.

I share my story to let you know the crickets sing for you too. Can you hear them? The chorus is stupendous! The music comforts the soul? The God who created their song is singing for you and desperately loves you? He is saying:

I love you.
I created you.
I maintain you.
I want you to be with me some day.
I died for you.

I rose again.
I came to save you.
There is more to life than just this.

It takes ears of faith and a listening heart to hear the song. Most of us are too preoccupied with:

our lives

our plans

our dreams

our schedules

our independence

We are too preoccupied to even think about shiny black bugs chirping away. But they are. God gave them the talent to sing lovely harmonies at night, harmonies for you to hear, harmonies of His love expressed to you. We just have to stop and notice this amazing world to find the master Musician who takes care of it all - who takes care of *us* all.

Most of us race through life never knowing the Musician. His music is everywhere, in the beautiful changing colors of the leaves, in the delicate fluttering butterflies that emerge from ugly caterpillars, in stupendous rainbows that hover above us and in the helpless first cry of a newborn baby. He is the *obvious* One, but the One most people don't see, don't hear, don't seek, don't believe and, frankly - just ignore. They are not interested, and it breaks His heart.

We live and move in *His* world that He put together and maintains – crickets and all. We didn't put anything in place – *He* did, and He did it perfectly, meticulously to the last detail.

We squirm, reason and rationalize to remove Him from our lives with our own melodies when it is so simple to "hear" childlike tunes – tunes about a trust, faith in the unseen spiritual realm.

People say He is a crutch – a fairy tale. I say He is a Father, a Guide, Someone who sent His Son to rescue us and die for all our sins so that He could be in relationship with us – not a religion and its dry, binding rules – but our personal Creator. He is the one who made us, designed our eyes to see, our ears to hear and gave us eyelashes to keep the dust from our eyes. He is the one who bent our elbow at just the right place so that we could brush our teeth and comb our hair – hold our babies.

He created us as spiritual beings with the ability to believe – reach Him – be in relationship with Him through faith. I had emptiness in my life just like the rest of us – some unmet need that only He could fill. I just didn't know it and tried to fill my life with other dreams and relationships that didn't truly satisfy.

Sooner or later, we get to the end of it all and realize we're missing something. That something is Jesus Christ. He is the only One who can stop that ache and the question, "Is this all there is?" to truly satisfy. That satisfaction feels like deep joy and contentment, security and peace – peace with ourselves and peace with God. I found that He truly is enough, and I look forward to meeting Him some day.

Crickets sing every night. Can you hear them? Open your ears. Open your spiritual ears. Crickets are singing all around you – not just a loud noise from ugly bugs – but a love song.

God's song for you:

He is there.

He knows you.

He loves you.

Remember, He didn't *have* to make the crickets sing at night.

Epilogue

> For God so loved the world that he gave his one
> and only Son. . . . John 3:16

My life is now full of peace and joy, hope and stability.

God did fulfill many of those chapters in my life. I am married to a wonderful loving and faithful husband who I now know can't possibly meet my every need. But I *have* met the real Knight in Shining Armor Who can, and He is stronger than any human relationship could ever be. I am surrounded by loving children who all live within a few miles of my house. I watch my grandchildren every day and get to see them dance in the living room or swim in the "deep, deep" part of the pool. My life is rich with love from my children and grandchildren who also love the Lord, but I am also part of a loving family of believers who support and share my struggles spiritually. I will share eternity with all these precious loved ones who know the Lord Jesus in a personal way.

Now my journey is focused on Jesus Christ and His plan for me. There are no more monsters hiding because He has conquered them all and keeps me safe in His loving arms.

Every day I experience a green pasture as He has taught me to:

Stay in the now.

Speak the truth.

Don't analyze.

Do the task for the day.

I learned that *the answer* is God, and that He is in total control - always.

The teaching job has been fulfilled in a marvelous way outside the restraints of a rigid school system to allow, perhaps, a different type of reading instruction to help many children. And many children *have* been helped by this wonderful curriculum that God gave to me.

Perhaps some of the mystery involving the turn of events in my math position at my school is explained in the following:

> I take several kids to vacation Bible school summer after summer.
>
> I have the opportunity to talk about God's love for them every day in my preschool.
>
> I teach them to pray about their "little worries" like losing their favorite toy.
>
> They see God answering their little prayers.
>
> I teach them to trust God when they are afraid.
>
> I see their eyes sparkle as they dance to familiar Jesus' songs.

In God's economy there is just no comparison where the true value lies in His eyes.

As I learned to walk in the Spirit, I followed behind while God not only gave me this wonderful reading program, but led one step at a time setting up a small reading group to test the program, getting The Ohio State University research department involved, collecting formal data for better sales to public schools and putting the appropriate people in authority to guide me along the way.

God has done a marvelous work in my life to heal all the brokenness that I experienced from my own lost condition and my false notions of life.

His song begins with love - eternal love - God's love for *you*. *You* can have a relationship with God, as well, through His Son, Jesus Christ. He wants *you* to know that:

- He loves *you* immeasurably, passionately.
  John 3:16 - For God so loved the world that he gave his one and only Son that whosoever believes in Him shall not perish but have eternal life.

- You are *separated* from Him because of *your* sin (imperfections) and will be eternally lost when *you* die.
  Romans 3:23 - for all have sinned and fall short of the glory of God.

- Jesus came to Earth to die and pay for *all your* sins.
  I Corinthians 15:3 - . . . that Christ died for our sins according to the Scriptures . . . .

- If you place your faith/trust in Jesus' finished work on the cross where He shed His blood so long ago and later rose from the dead, *He will save you.*
  Ephesians 2:8, 9 - For it is by grace you have been saved, through faith - and this is not from yourselves, it is the *gift* of God— not by works, so that no one can boast.

  Romans 10:9 – That if you confess with your mouth, Jesus is Lord, and believe in your heart (not intellect) that God raised him from the dead, you will be saved.

You can have a personal relationship with the God of Heaven. He loves *you*, created *you* and knows *you*. He will give you love, peace, purpose and fill your heart with hope. This relationship is possible because of His Son's sacrifice on the cross – the Lord Jesus Christ.

If this is the desire of your heart, you can pray a simple prayer and ask Him to forgive you and to become your Lord and Savior.

A suggested prayer might be:

Dear God, I know that You love me. I know that I have sinned against You. I understand that my sin has separated me from You. I believe that Jesus Christ died and paid for all my sins by shedding His blood on the cross. I believe He rose again on the third day and is in Heaven with You right now. I receive this payment for my sin as a free gift and I give my life to You. Thank you for saving me and making me Your child.

If you find your God through Jesus Christ - the Creator of all things - the purpose of this book will have been accomplished and another cricket song will begin.

CPSIA information can be obtained at www.ICGtesting.com
Printed in the USA
BVOW05s1841161014

371143BV00001B/8/P